WHEN YOU HEAR HOOFBEATS
THINK OF A ZEBRA

TALKS ON SUFISM

WHEN YOU HEAR HOOFBEATS THINK OF A ZEBRA

BY SHEMS FRIEDLANDER

PERENNIAL LIBRARY

Harper & Row, Publishers, New York
Cambridge, Philadelphia, San Francisco, Washington
London, Mexico City, São Paulo, Singapore, Sydney

To my son,
NURI

TYPOGRAPHY: Fine Lines Graphic Services, Inc., NYC

First PERENNIAL LIBRARY edition published 1987.

LIBRARY OF CONGRESS CATALOG CARD NUMBER: 86-45657

ISBN: 0-06-096128-7

87 88 89 90 91 MPC 10 9 8 7 6 5 4 3 2 1

CONTENTS

INTRODUCTION
by Daniel Goleman

"You can plan for a hundred years, but you don't know what will happen in the next moment."

Just as the human predicament transcends all boundaries of time and place, the eternal facts of life revolve around problems of living that every person must face, the meaning of life and the inevitability of death.

The ancient spiritual traditions of all the world deal with just how one ought to confront these verities. The use of stories to make these points is as old in human history as are man's attempts to grapple with these questions.

Stories have a unique power, an ability to make their points without marshalling the mental resistance that more sharply reasoned rational appeals often raise. Knowledge is best transmitted through rational means, speaking directly to the mind. But wisdom strikes to the heart when it is carried in a tale.

There are many books that collect wisdom stories. But such collections leave out something crucial, these stories are used most artfully when told to a specific person or group to make a specific point. Timing and context give them their special power. To hear the stories out of context is to miss their full meaning.

We are fortunate to have these tales in their context, with the points they embroider and elaborate. These living moments are a rare offering, one that not only shows how teaching stories teach, but which also offers those same lessons in life to the reader.

Tales such as those used by Shems Friedlander have recently come into popularity among psychotherapists in the West. The pioneer in using stories as part of therapy was Milton Erickson, a psychiatrist and master hypnotist who developed to a fine art the ability to tell, at just the right moment, exactly the tale his patient needed to hear. Telling a story is such an artful way to instruct because it is so disarming: the tale seems to be about someone else, and yet the mind automatically draws the parallels to one's own life. It is easier to hear about another person's dilemma than it is to look hard at one's own quirks.

The use of these stories for therapy arrives with a new scientific appreciation of the intuitive powers they set free. These tales speak the language of the unconscious, the language of metaphor and emotion, of imagination and healing. Insights made through stories do not alarm the psychic defenses. The rational mind does not quite perceive their challenge, and so does not resist. Thus these tales slip through the ego's defense, penetrating the mental prisons built by fixed habits of thought and perception.

Perhaps most powerfully, stories can suggest an altogether different understanding of the situation, and show a creative alternative to what may have seemed a hopeless bind. The title of this book alludes to that ability of tales to teach a new way of seeing things, of thinking about them, and of responding. "When You Hear Hoofbeats Think of a Zebra," the title enjoins; implicit in that advice is: stop automatically thinking of horses everytime there are hoofbeats.

In other words, think in a new way. That is the antidote to what has been called "psychosclerosis," hardening of the attitudes. Habits — ruts in the psyche — lock us into mental prisons. Just the right story can suggest, very gently, a key to unlocking the door. Such an insight can lead to a small step toward change. But, as Milton Erickson saw, small changes lead to big ones. In this sense, teaching tales can be transforming.

Modern psychology has come to have a deep respect for the lessons that are imparted by stories. They instruct the part of the mind that knows without saying, the part that is closest to the heart's own truth. As such, modern therapy is borrowing the tools of an ancient psychology. And the teaching talks Shems

Friedlander shares here with us depict that psychology in action.

There are, of course, psychologies and there are psychologies. And then there is the perennial psychology, the one that addresses the ultimate questions of life. This ultimate psychology stems from a different mode of knowing than does ordinary psychology; it requires an inner knowing. From such a sense of inner certainty flows faith. Sheikh Muzaffer al-Halveti al-Jerrahi has said, "Faith in Allah is an innoculation against the diseases of the world."

It is in dealing with these "diseases of the world" — with greed, lust, anger, jealousy, self-pity, and all the other roots of heaviness of heart — that the perennial psychology is distinct from ordinary psychology. This is a psychology that begins where modern psychologies end; that deals with the largest issues of life rather than the smallest.

Although modern psychology proceeds from the chauvinistic assumption that psychology began within the last century in Europe and America, the truth is that psychology is a human endeavor that has been with us since recorded history. It has taken many, many forms. In ancient times, those forms were religious: there is a psychology at the inner core of all the great spiritual teachings. Judaism has its psychology, the Kaballah; Christianity has its esoteric teachings, and Islam has Sufism. Each of these is a fully developed theory of the human mind and heart, of the forces that limit and bind the human spirit, and of the path to liberation.

In this sense, Shems Friedlander's book can be read as a psychology text — a text of the perennial psychology, which is to say, a book of lessons for living. He speaks to the verities, the eternal issues and lessons, of qualities such as patience, friendship, heedfulness and right living. It is such teachings that our modern psychologies, sad to say, for the most part lack.

Shems Friedlander tells a parable that it is both sobering and terribly important. It says, in short, that we are each given three days to live, and two have passed.

GLOSSARY OF TERMS

adab Manners, etiquette, behavior, the proper conduct and discipline of the Sufi in relation to his sheikh and associate Sufis; the mode of right action, spiritual courtesy.

adhan The call to prayer.

alhamdulillah All praise is due to Allah.

alim One trained in the religious sciences.

Allahu akbar Allah is the Greatest.

arif Gnostic, adept, one who has been given mystical knowledge, is acquainted with the Divine Being.

asma, esma (Turk.) Name. *Al-asma'al-husna:* The 99 most beautiful Names of Allah.

basmala The opening phrase of the Quranic suras except sura ir Rahman. *Bismillah ir-rahman ir-rahim:* In the Name of Allah the Compassionate, the Merciful.

chilla, chille (Turk.) 1001 day retreat of the Mevlevi dervishes.

destur (Turk.) Permission.

dervish, darwish (Pers.) Follower of the Sufi path.

dhikr Remembrance, recollection of Allah through the invocation of His Names.

dua A supplication. A personal prayer at the end of the prescribed prayer.

faqir, pl. **fuqura** A general term for a dervish.

Fatiha, al The Opener. The chapter with which the Quran opens.

hadith Tradition going back to the Prophet. Narration, account; report of the actions and sayings of the Prophet transmitted through trustworthy intermediaries.

hadith qudsi A tradition in which Allah speaks in the first person to the Prophet. A Sacred account; non-Quranic Divine Word revealed to the Prophet.

hajj Ritual pilgrimage to Makkah.

halqa 'Circle' around the sheikh, spiritual guide; a circle of dhikr devotees, dervishes.

haqiqa, al The Reality.

Haqq, al Truth. The Real; the Divine Reality as distinguished from Creation. Sufi term for Allah and as distinguished from *haqiqa*.

haydariyyah Dervish vest derived from Imam Ali whose name was also Haydar.

Hayy The Everliving. One of the names and attributes of Allah.

hoja A teacher.

Hu He. When referring to Allah as He. A *dhikr* repetition.

iftar Break of fast.

ijaza License or diploma testifying to the holder's link with a *tariqa*, order and its founder.

ikhwan Brethren, fellow members of a dervish order.

imam Leader in public worship.

insha'Allah Godwilling, Allah willing.

istihara Asking Allah to show the right course of action to be revealed in a dream or through some other sign.

khalifa Vicar, deputy; the initiating leader of a branch of an order nominated by the sheikh.

khalwa, halwat (Turk.) Seclusion, retreat; a place of seclusion or retreat. The act of total abandonment in desire of the Divine Presence.

khirqa, hirka (Turk.) A dervish's patched garment, symbolizing his vows of obedience to the rule of his order.

kiyaam Standing. As in *dhikr kiyaam*, standing dhikr.

mangal Brazier.

ma'rifa Intuitive knowledge, gnostic wisdom.

mathnawi, masnavi (Turk.) Poem in couplets. Also 'Masnavi' title of the celebrated epic poem by Rumi.

mihrab A niche in the wall of a mosque indicating the *qibla*, direction of Makkah and of prayer.

muezzin Chanter of the call to prayer.

Muhammad The Prophet of Islam, may the peace and blessings of Allah be upon him.

muhib Lover. Affiliate to a dervish order.

murid An 'aspirant', disciple, novice.

murshid Sufi sheikh, guide or director.

nafs Self, ego, desires. The lower self, the animal spirit. The *nafs* act as a veil separating the dervish from Allah. Sufism deals with seven stages of refinements of the *nafs*.

pir Elder, used for the Sufi superior and founder in Turkish dervish orders.

post Sheepskin throne of a dervish.

post-nishin The sheepskin throne of the sheikh of the order, often dyed blue or red.

Quran The Holy Book of Islam.

qutb, kutub (Turk.) Lit. axis, pivot. Head of the spiritual hierarchy of the world. The highest station in the Sufi hierarchy of Saints.

rasul Apostle.

salat Islamic ritual prayer.

sharia The path to be followed–the exoteric revelation, Islamic jurisprudence.

sheikh Spiritual head, teacher of a dervish order.

silsila A chain, and so a lineage, a chain of spiritual descent tracing all the *khalifas* and sheikhs of a dervish order.

sufi An Islamic mystic.

sura A chapter of the Quran.

taj Crown, term used for the high-crowned turban worn by dervish sheikhs and *khalifas.*

taqiya Dervish skull cap or other headgear.

tariq & tariqa A way, the term for the Sufi path; a mystical method, system or school of guidance for traversing and following the Path.

taslimiyat Submission to Allah, to the sheikh.

tasawwuf Islamic mysticism: English formulation Sufism, derived from *suf* 'wool'.

tasbih, tesbih (Turk.) The repetition of Allah's Name often using prayer beads to maintain the count of the repetition. Often refers directly to the prayer beads themselves as well as the daily practices of the dervish.

tawhid The declaration of Unity and Unicity of Allah as expressed by the phrase: *la ilaha illa Allah,* 'There is no god but Allah.'

tekke Dervish center, meeting lodge, hospice.

tenure The white robe of the Mevlevi dervish that also symbolizes his shroud.

umra The small pilgrimage to Makkah.

vizier A minister.

wird Litanies composed of strung together remembrance formulae emblematic of a dervish order.

THE ZEBRA

 When we hear hoofbeats, do we think of a zebra? Probably not. Because we usually do everything the way we've always done it. I'm interested in how we perceive reality and how we gain the knowledge to accomplish this. Islam and Sufism ask us to gain knowledge. To have knowledge of Allah it is necessary to have knowledge of ourselves. If we truly know ourselves, then we will know Allah. If Allah allows us to know Him, we might know ourselves.

This body we live in is a kingdom and a grave. It is a kingdom where our heart resides. It is the grave of our soul. Our heart has the spiritual faculty of knowing Allah. Through this body we experience the world, we travel through this world like a traveler in the desert, and no one remains here. When it is their time, all the prophets and beings endowed with divine grace and knowledge, regardless of their achievement and station, will go. He who created them will also take them, whether they are willing to go or not. This power that brought us here will remove us from here. This power of Allah not only created us, but created everyone and everything we love; whether it be a man, woman, or flower, it is His creation.

To understand Sufism, we have to understand that Allah, who created the heavens and the earth and all in between, also created us. If we can fathom and accept that Allah created each of us, then we know that He has created everyone who is on this planet. We are not just something that happened; each of us is a miracle. If we understood this, we would not take ourselves for granted.

1

This body is like the earth. Our bones are like mountains. Our belly is like the sea. Our flesh is like the dust and the mud. The hair that grows on us is like plants, and the skin from which this hair grows is like arable land, and the area of our body where hair does not grow is akin to saline soil. Our sadness is like darkness and our laughter like sunlight. Sleep is brother to death. Our childhood is like spring, our youth like summer. Our maturity is like the autumn, our old age like the winter of our life. All of our movements are like the stars moving in the sky.

In this universe that Allah has created, we are His supreme miracle. If we walk through this life totally unconscious, half-asleep, then how can we thank Him? A real dervish, if for a moment he forgets Allah, will perform a total ablution.

We have to study ourselves, study our actions. If anger becomes the ruler of our kingdom, we must see this anger. If laziness steps to the front, we must recognize this laziness. Then again, deceit or gossip may take over and become the ruler of our kingdom. We must observe all these traits within ourselves. Here, within this universe that we call ourselves, is the zoo of man, and there is no admission charge. Each day we can observe how the angry wolf comes forward, how the scorpion stings, or how the monkey just takes over and chatters and plays.

All the animals that exist in the world, besides having certain functions for man's benefit, also exist to show us various parts of our nature. People want to know the mysteries of life. They want the hidden secrets of life revealed to them. Well, here they are! We just have to open our eyes. Every fruit, every vegetable has a different taste, yet when you cook them all in one pot, there is one taste. Here is a mystery.

Not only are we obligated to seek knowledge, we must also understand how to behave in life. We will never understand this unless we observe ourselves in daily life. Observe ourselves, and not try immediately to change, but to say, "Ah, this lazy one again,

2

how easily he got angry." We must first try to recognize all the faults within us, in order to change them into qualities, in order to become our own shepherd.

Yoga means union and comes from the root word *yunakti*, "he yokes." Yoga is a self-imposed discipline. The real meaning of yoga is to accept the discipline, to be obedient to something outside ourselves in order to grow.

A man was wounded in battle, but he didn't let his friends draw the arrow out of him. First he wanted to know who the archer was, what he looked like, and where he was standing when he shot the arrow. He wanted to know the type of bow and the length of the arrow. As he discussed all these things, he died.

This is how we are in life. We must pull out the arrow of useless thoughts, throw it away, and discard the toys of our mind before it is too late.

We make our prayers and roll our beads. If we do it mechanically, we don't change, and then we argue that there is something missing in the Path. How do we change ourselves? When we say *Bismillah*, in the Name of Allah, before we eat and then just gobble down the food, never thinking of Allah, we come to the end of the meal feeling stuffed and only know that we have eaten a lot of food. If we say *Bismillah* knowing that we are putting the *Nur*, Light of Allah, into the food, and if we eat this food with the idea that the food will nourish us so that we may be strong to pray to Allah and thank Him, then we are eating correctly. If we dress not out of vanity and not for fashion, then we are dressing correctly.

What is this life, that passes so quickly and in a moment is gone? An old dervish in Madinah once said to me that life is a gift that consists of three days and two are gone. No matter how much money you have, regardless of how much influence you have in this world, you cannot bring those days back. We have one day left, and in that remaining day are we going to seek the pleasures of the world that we know are so temporary? Can we not put the love of Allah in our hearts before that heart becomes dust? For dust it will become. And for those who could never have enough of big houses and acres of land, one day they will have to be satisfied with six feet of earth.

How can we remove these veils . . . before our eyes can no longer see and our ears no longer hear? There is a time limit. It is Allah's secret, and it is different for each one of us. But our intelligence tells us there is a time limit. This very same intelligence that doesn't even see we are dying at every moment. Then one day we have gray in our hair, wrinkles on our skin. If all this is happening on the outside, it must also be happening inside our bodies. We will go. All it takes is one moment, and we will never be able to see with these eyes again or smell with this nose or hear with these ears or breathe with these lungs or walk with these legs.

A companion of Prophet Muhammad hired a man to come to him every day and remind him of death. The man did this. Years went by, and each day the man would come and say, "There is death."

One day he was told, "You have done a good job, but I no longer need your services."

"I have also been reminded of my own death each day that I reminded you," said the man, "and it has been important in my life. Why do you stop now?"

"Because Allah has put gray in my beard, and this gray hair reminds me that there is an end to this life."

How can we not get caught by the world as much as we do? These are the things Sufism deals with that people don't talk to you about, but this is Sufism.

Sufism is finding fishes of gold in rivers of sand. So we must do practical things. How do we do that? When we get up in the morning, when we open our eyes, do we say: "It's too early! I'm tired, go back to sleep," or: "Thank you, Allah, for allowing me another day, a beginning of a new day."

4

This is the month of Rajab, the first of four holy months in the Islamic calendar. Last year I heard my sheikh say, "This may be your last Rajab." It was his last Rajab. No one knows the moment of his death. All of us will have our last Rajab. Yet like children we continue to pursue and desire the world's shiny toys.

Every morning when we get up, we must remember two things—Allah and our death. If we remember Allah and if we remember our death, then our lives will be different. There is a fixed time limit of life for each one of us that Allah has kept a secret. If we remember our death, then we will also remember that all things and all beings are temporary. If we remember Allah we will do everything in divine thoughtfulness, kindness, and understanding. Because we will understand that He not only created us, but He created everyone and everything that we see. If there are wrongs occurring in this world that we don't like, then the way to right them is by curing ourselves, each one of us individually. Why do you think that in a supposedly civilized world there are terrorism, war, hijacking, and hostages? All these and more exist because man has forgotten Who created him. Man has forgotten Allah. Man has forgotten where he came from, where he is, and where he is going.

I heard an appalling thing the other day. Do you know that in the ten years after the end of the Vietnam war, more Vietnam veterans committed suicide than were killed on the battlefield? This says something about our society. We are that society.

The message from Allah often comes through opposites. If we don't see the bad, we will never see the good. If we only see health, He shows us illness. If we only see the living, we'll take life for granted, so He shows us death. How can we understand that every single thing in our life is a message revealed by Allah for us to understand Allah? There is a *hadith*, an action or a saying of the Prophet Muhammad, that says whatever object strikes you could never have missed you and whatever missed you could never have struck you. Everything is destined, everything is a trace of Allah, a trace of His knowledge.

So, after we've opened our eyes and we've thanked Allah and we've remembered Him, we remember our death, and by remembering our death we know that nothing will last, nothing! How many have come before us and are no longer here? Those we have known and those we haven't known, greater people than us, and yet we pass each day with arrogance. We are blinded and caught by what the world seems to be offering, which is only some temporary pabulum.

Not long ago Sheikh Muzaffer el-Jerrahi, the head of the Halveti-Jerrahi Order of Dervishes, departed the earth. I am sad that he is gone. I'm sad for myself more than for him. Who will replace the inner work that he did every day? How many people will it take to equal one of his prayers? No one person can do it. It is the job of everyone who knew him and loved him to do a little bit more in their lives, and if everyone contributes, we could possibly achieve the great work that he performed and accomplished. He was a man, and no man in this world is without problems.

Two dervishes met on the road very early one morning. Each had a huge bale of firewood on his back. The sultan passed and saw them. Many hours later the sultan returned near this spot and saw that the two men were still standing, shouldering their heavy loads and talking.

"Who are these men?" asked the sultan.

"They are dervishes, O sultan," said one of his attendants, "and when they are with one another the burdens of the world disappear."

Sufism is made up of a group of people. It is a form of togetherness. The mirrors we use in life are false. The only true mirror is the heart of a human being that reflects divine light. Therefore, when we are with others, we not only have the opportunity to learn about them, we can also learn about ourselves. Can we get a true

6

reflection from mirrors backed by silver and darkness? No! Only when we try to see ourselves in the hearts of our companions do we see ourselves as we truly are.

We must introduce adventure into our lives. We must extricate ourselves from this sensation of swimming in pea soup through the day. We have to do things differently, simple things. If you stir your coffee with your right hand, stir it with your left hand. If you do the dishes in ten minutes, then wash them in twenty minutes. Do them at half the rate of your normal speed. See yourself standing there. From everything we observe we can learn, from the simplest, ordinary things we can learn ten thousand other things. Stand in front of the dishes. Here is a dish. There was a potter, some clay. Where did the clay come from? What kind of earth, color, glaze, kiln? Everything can be traced all the way back to Allah. You lift a glass and know that your body has taken a shape other than the shape it was a second before. You can feel the warmth or cold of something in your hands. Or when you shake hands with someone, you hold his hand a second longer: "Here I am, *now* I greet you." Because unless we can become a real person, and become aware of the things that Allah has presented us, how can we help other people? How can we help ourselves?

This is not an easy life. This life is filled with hardships and pleasures, but it is temporary. A farmer in Anatolia had a wife and adolescent son. His wife always complained that they were poor, their house needed a new roof, the barn was broken down, and they had no horse to help with the plowing. Early one morning the man and his son looked toward the field, and beside a large oak tree stood the most beautiful thing they had ever seen.

It was a large white horse with perfect proportions. They tied and fed the horse. They were happy. His wife came out and said, "Look for markings, it is a rich man's horse." There were no markings.

"We can sell the horse," the wife said, "and with the money we can fix the roof, buy a wagon, rebuild the barn, and have something left over for our old age."

"I will not sell the horse," said the man.

"If you don't, I will leave you," said the wife, and went into the house.

Now let me tell you a little about the man. The townspeople and his wife thought he was becoming senile. Whenever something occurred, good or bad, he would say, "Maybe it's a blessing, maybe it's a curse, only Allah knows." Whatever befell him, that's what he would say. That's what he said when the townspeople gathered on his land to see the horse and told him what good fortune he had.

And that's what he said to his wife after she told him that he should sell or she would leave. The next morning, he began building a corral for the horse. His wife became angry. She went to her sister down the road. The man shrugged his shoulders and said, "Maybe it's a blessing, maybe a curse, only Allah knows."

The story of the beautiful horse traveled from village to village, town to town, and finally to the capital city where the sultan, a lover of horses, heard it. He called his lieutenant and told him to go to the farmer and offer him a bag of gold for the horse. A vast sum of money.

"What if he won't sell?" asked the lieutenant.

"Of course he will," said the sultan, "he is poor. This is a fortune."

"But," the lieutenant insisted, "what if he won't sell?"

"Then kill him," said the sultan, "and bring me the horse."

The sultan's soldiers arrived at the farmer's house. The horse was as beautiful as they had been told, and the lieutenant offered the farmer the bag of gold for the horse.

"Thank you," said the farmer, "but I don't want to sell."

The lieutenant asked the farmer to walk with him. He liked the old man, who reminded him of his father.

"Please take the money," the lieutenant said.

8

"No," the farmer said.

"My orders are to kill you and take the horse if you won't sell it to me."

"The horse is not for sale."

"Please, this will be your death."

"Maybe it's a blessing, maybe a curse, only Allah knows."

The lieutenant said he had an errand in another village, but would return in a few days. He begged the farmer to think about selling the horse.

The townspeople gathered and started to argue with the farmer.

"You will be rich!"

"Maybe it's a blessing, maybe a curse, only Allah knows."

"If you don't sell the horse, the soldiers will kill you, so you will lose the horse either way."

"Maybe it's a blessing, maybe a curse, only Allah knows."

That night the farmer had a dream. Maybe something in the dream woke him. It was around 3 A.M. and he went outside. There was a mist. The horse was beautiful, moving in and out of the mist, disappearing and reappearing. As the farmer moved closer, he felt something special, extraordinary, in every part of his body. He remembered old teachings which said that God took the first breath of His day at this time. He felt touched by God, filled with light, washed clean of imperfection, and that feeling stayed with him.

The horse looked magnificent, his breath steaming from his nostrils into the mist.

Later that morning the farmer's son decided to ride the horse. He rode bareback through the forest and past fields. He felt wonderful, the wind caressing his face and pulling at strands of his hair. He wrapped his arms around the horse's neck. He was at one with the horse until the horse stepped into a hole, throwing the boy high into the air. Falling, the boy broke both his legs.

The townspeople found him and carried him home.

"You didn't listen to us," they said to the farmer. "If you had sold the horse, this wouldn't have happened. Now your son has two broken legs."

"Maybe it's a blessing, maybe it's a curse, only Allah knows," the farmer replied.

The next morning, the farmer looked outside and saw a terrible sight. In fact, he saw nothing. The horse was gone.

The townspeople said, "You could have sold him for money, and you didn't. So your son went riding and broke both his legs. Now you don't even have the horse."

"Maybe it's a blessing, maybe it's a curse, only Allah knows," said the farmer.

"The soldiers will come back," said the townspeople, "and they won't believe you when you say the horse disappeared. They'll torture you, and then they'll kill you."

"Maybe it's a blessing, maybe it's a curse, only Allah knows," said the farmer.

The soldiers didn't return. War had broken out. All the young men were called into the army, except for the farmer's son with his two broken legs.

"You're lucky," the townspeople said to the farmer. "We will never see our sons again. You will have someone to care for you in old age, but we will be alone."

"I've told you before," said the farmer. "Don't you understand? Maybe it's a blessing, maybe it's a curse. Only Allah knows."

How do we use our hardships and pleasures? If we are sitting here in this moment, can we see ourselves, become aware of our breathing, change our voice? Our voice, everything in life, is an instrument we can use.

Why is it that every time we hear hoofbeats, we think of a horse? Because we have been conditioned, and in that conditioning we have fallen asleep. In that state of sleep we have forgotten Allah. In that moment of forgetting Allah, we are capable of doing anything. But when we are in the state of remembering

10

Allah, in that moment we can only do good.

It is easy and interesting to discuss the history of Sufism. We can tell stories about the great saints and teachers, what they did, how they suffered or remembered Allah, but the real question each of us must ask and face is this: How do we live *our* lives? When we pray, are we thinking about getting it over quickly so we can get on with what we believe is more urgent in life? Are we always caught up in doing what is urgent and not what is important in life? When we look at our lives, can we see what really matters? What is most important? How can we raise our children in this world? We have a responsibility toward them. If we become closer to Allah, they become closer to Allah.

It is really necessary to act. But action is not *just* five prayers a day, which perhaps was a lot easier in the days of the Prophet Muhammad than it is now. Because the moment you step up out of that prayer, the world is right there either to dangle some shiny object in your face or pluck at you from some unknown place in order to seize your attention. And we are willing! I'm not saying that we shouldn't enjoy certain pleasures in life that are allowed. But where are we then? If we could realize that the moment we turn on the television, the television is turning us off. If we can just say, "I'm turning on the television, and the television is turning me off," how long will we watch? There are good things to watch, but maybe while we're watching television or going to the movies, we can roll our beads. We don't have to give all our attention to what is outside. It doesn't require all our attention. Actually, it requires much less attention than we imagine. We can have a meaningless conversation with someone at work and still retain something of ourselves, and with that something remember Allah. The conversation may be necessary within the confines of our job, but what is not necessary is to give ourselves totally to it.

We are all, no matter how old or how young, in the winter of our lives. And the Bektashi dervishes say that the winter sun is a lie.

11

Please, for your own sake, for the sake of those whom you love, remember Him. Not just the Name, but He who is Named. Not just remembering the Name Allah, but also always remembering all the manifestations of Allah — the earth and all the planets and all the galaxies and all the universes and all they contain, these only exist because Allah has created them and continuously sustains them in every shape and form. Know yourself always and everywhere, and remember Allah.

Whatever you see can be traced all the way back to Him. Here we have a glass vase. I don't know who made this vase. Someone blew the glass into this shape. I can believe that someone blew the glass into this vase without ever knowing that person, without ever having seen him. Then why can't I believe that everything I see was created by Allah? When I look at a piece of sculpture, and I think, "What a nice piece of sculpture, the sculptor is a good artist," why then can I not take the thought further and realize that the sculptor himself was created by Allah?

Can I battle my laziness? Must I always give in to my body's desires? Well, I say, I have this thing to do, but first I'm going to take a little rest. Body, you're tired. I'll rest awhile, then I'll do it. Can't we say, No! First I'll do it, then I'll rest awhile. How far can we push ourselves? How can we reach the state of working with joy? A state of no reluctance to perform tasks, whether they be sweeping a floor, washing the dishes, painting a room, or anything that we are called on to do in this life. If we performed the task and remembered Allah in the process, then we have joy. But usually we do things in order to be rid of them as quickly as possible so that we can go on and do something else that we can be rid of as quickly as possible, or maybe not do at all, or waste more time and energy in finding ways not to do things than it would take us to do them.

Allah has given us free will. It is up to us to use it. No sheikh can do that for you. No sheikh can do your *tesbih*, prayer beads, for you or pray for you or work with joy for you or remember Allah for you. No one can do this for you. Each of us has to do this by himself.

Why don't we tremble when we hear the Name of Allah? Why don't we weep? My sheikh used to say, "If we don't weep, then we should weep *because* we don't weep."

All of us, let us pray and ask Allah for help. Everyone, close your eyes, right at this moment, close them! Snap! That's how quickly death can come. That quickly! And it is only the gift of Allah that allows you to open them again. There are some people on this planet who at the very moment we closed our eyes, closed theirs and could not reopen them.

Allah is most Generous and most Forgiving. He is most Generous because He loves His creation, and He is most Forgiving because He knows that we need a Lord with forgiveness. If we do something wrong, we should then ask for forgiveness. Don't just take it for granted and say, "I've done something wrong. Now I don't ever have to do anything right again" or "Well, I haven't done my prayers for two weeks, so now I don't have to do them anymore. I haven't done my *tesbih*, so why should I continue?" CONTINUE! If you have forgotten Allah, remember Him. We remember Him because we have forgotten Him.

Somehow . . . somehow we have to get through this fog. We have to help each other do that. We have to keep remembering and reminding each other.

"Make them remember." This was told to the Prophet Muhammad. But it is also told to everyone. Farid-ud-din Attar, the Sufi master who wrote *The Conference of the Birds*, said: "Be in the company of those who remind you of Allah." We see what happens when we are not in that company. We have had enough experiences, and we are not strong enough to be alone in this world.

These are some of the things I've been thinking about since Sheikh Muzaffer passed away, and I wanted to share them with you.

13

THE WINTER SUN IS A LIE

Man is a miracle of Allah, and within this lifetime man has the possibility of fulfilling the joy of that miracle.

This world is not an easy place. It is a place that we enter with pain, and the only way we can leave it is with death. The Quran says that when we perform good deeds, they will be counted and when we perform forbidden deeds, we will be punished.

Imam Ali says: "Here, the wealthy are often involved with vice and sin, and the poor are often involved with sorrow and calamities." This is where we are. But Allah has created us for a greater purpose, and no other living being on this planet has been endowed with the same possibilities.

Allah says that He created man for Himself and the entire universe for man. The question is, where are *we* in that universe? What do we really understand of it? How awake are we within the conditions of our daily life? Or do we walk through this life as somnambulistic meanderers? What do we see during the day in order to gain a certain knowledge and understanding of ourselves?

We find a place in a room, a room that we know at home or a room that we don't know somewhere else, and we find a little space that is comfortable to us, and we continue to go right to that place every time we enter the room. This is how man is!

But there's also the possibility of the adventure, to sit in another place and to see the room and the people in it from another point of view. How often do we take our own house, the place we live in, and move the furniture around so that it's not exactly the same

15

every time, and we come home and say: "Ah, so this is my place!" Or is it that everything sits year after year in the same place? We don't change a picture. We don't change a chair. It all just stays there. We're like this, but I think we have to get into a more playful attitude with how we are with our lives, just to be able to see ourselves a little better.

Abdullah Al-Mubarak Al-Halveti was returning from *hajj*. He was on foot, and on the side of the road he saw a young boy who was playing with sand. The boy was building a huge sand castle, pushing the sand up with his hands and making a big mound. Then he would knock it down and as it all fell, he would begin to cry.

Approaching the boy, Abdullah thought, "Should I greet this boy? He's just a child." Then he remembered that the Prophet always greeted children, always greeted everyone. Abdullah said, "*As-salaam aleykum*, peace and blessings of Allah be upon you."

The boy, without looking up, said, "*Wa-aleykum as-salaam*, and peace and blessings of Allah be upon you, Abdullah Mubarak."

Abdullah Mubarak, taken aback, said, "How do you know my name?"

"Well," the boy replied, "I remember in the other world we were standing together in the same prayer line, and Allah called your name."

Abdullah Mubarak asked, "What are you doing playing in the sand?"

"I'm a child," the boy said. "This is what children do!"

"But," Abdullah Mubarak asked, "what is this strange game you are playing? Why do you build this mound of sand and after it is all built up, when it looks perfect, you break it down and then begin to cry?"

The boy answered, "When I build up the sand, it represents the heart of man and the unity of all men through the heart. When I destroy it, this heart breaks into thousands of little pieces and disperses, then there is no unity. At that point, I begin to cry."

Abdullah Mubarak said, "May I stay and have you as my teacher?" And he stayed with the boy.

It is through unity, through the unity of hearts, and through the brotherhood and friendship of people that true Sufism and true Islam are expressed. But if we are not a little conscious of ourselves and who we are, how we spend our time, then it is difficult to climb to a higher level and work from there.

A sultan once said, "I will give a bag of gold to anyone who has accomplished the most unusual thing." People came to the court with all kinds of accomplishments. One man had a friend hold a needle at one end of the courtyard. The man then took a thread and threw it a hundred feet through the air. It went through the eye of the needle. It was the most unusual thing, and the sultan gave him the bag of gold, saying, "You've accomplished a feat that I learned has taken you twenty years to perfect, and it is truly a remarkable feat, but it is useless. And because you've spent twenty years of your life accomplishing such a useless thing, I also give you one hundred lashes."

What we do in our lives for ourselves is important. But in those lives, we can also have the ambition to help others. You can spend twenty years of your life doing something very good and ac- complished, but it's of no real use if it only provides your bread and rent and a few pleasures. But if it does not provide for other greater possibilities, your time and your life will have been wasted.

Let us look at an example of what we do in life and whether or not it's possible to do things that can be helpful to other people. The help can even be indirect. You can be a writer and write something that someone reads and is so touched by something in your writing that he moves in a new direction. You can make clothes and put such love into them that when someone wears them, he will feel different.

When we cook a meal for someone, we think about where the

17

food came from, and we thank Allah for the food. Do we love the food, do we love the person we're cooking for, or is it just a task that we do because we have to do it?

There are lessons in everything. In preparing our food, where food comes from and being healthy enough to eat the food. There are millionaires in hospitals who can't take a drink of water.

Food comes from Allah. In it, there is a message. Something usually has to be removed from each piece of food that we eat. Either the skin, the bones, or a crust. Even if nothing has to be removed, the food is at least washed or inspected. Yet we come home from work, and never wash the anger from our bodies. We don't wash the tension from ourselves. We will immediately go to husband, wife, friend, or child, and embrace them before we remove that anger and tension and trouble of the day. Then we wonder why the relationship isn't working or why there are problems. The message is right there in that piece of food which nourishes us. But we have to learn to *see*.

The Sufi doesn't eat too much. If we are meditating or in *halwat*, retreat, we don't eat meat, because meat blocks us. So if we know that meat blocks us when we're in *halwat*, we also should know that it's going to block us in our daily life. Maybe we should eat less meat. That is also a message. If it is advised while we're in *halwat*, while we're in the place where we hope to become closer to Allah, that we should not eat much, then shouldn't we understand that it also means we should not overindulge in anything, whether it be food or talk, or whatever could become harmful to us?

Do we ask Allah to help us? This world which we enter through pain and leave through death is obviously a place where we have to ask Allah for help.

There was a man who studied with a sheikh for thirty years. Then he said to the sheikh, "Now I want to go out with your permission to see if I can also teach others what I have learned from you."

18

The sheikh said, "I'll ask you one question. If you can answer this question, I'll know that you are ready. It is not a question from the Quran," he added. "On your way back to your village," the sheikh went on, "will you pass a place where there are shepherds?"

The man said yes.

Then the sheikh asked, "As you walk by this place where there is a shepherd with his sheep, if five of his sheepdogs attacked you, what would you do?"

The man said, "I'd pick up a stone and throw it."

And the sheikh said, "You might hit one dog, but the other four would get you."

The man said, "Well, I would take a stick and try to keep them off."

And the sheikh said, "I say to you again that you might get one or even two, but the remainder of the dogs would certainly attack you. I can see that you are not yet ready to go out to teach others in your own village."

The man said, "O sheikh, at least tell me the answer."

The sheikh told him that if he called for the shepherd, the shepherd would come from his tent, and call each of the dogs by its name, and the dogs would turn away from the attack.

Then the sheikh said, "In this world there are people who will attack you like those dogs, and if you try to fight them off, they will win. But if you call their owner, if you call the One who created them, then He will call them by name and will protect you."

We call Allah when we are in trouble. But do we call Him when we are not in trouble? Sufis do a *dhikr kiyaam*, standing remembrance. The real *dhikr kiyaam* is when we stand up in our prayer to Allah. That is the *kiyaam*. The *kiyaam* in the *dhikr* refers to when you stand in front of Allah. It is that *kiyaam* we are standing in at the moment of prayer. It is the *kiyaam* of Moses on the mountain.

The days, the weeks, and the months pass, and my sheikh is gone. Sheikh Muzaffer Efendi was a great man in this world, and

I miss him. As I thought of Efendi, I saw that each of us had his own perspective of his death, from wherever we were at that moment, however we heard it, however we experienced it in the days or weeks that followed. I'll share what my experience was like, because as you yourself were shocked when you heard the news of that dark Tuesday, so was I. I had seen him in Istanbul only a few weeks before, and thought he looked well. He wore a new brown suit and greeted everyone with great joy. He sat straight and looked wonderful. I thought he looked healthier than he had been in years. And that night there was the most wonderful *dhikr Allah*.

Then, a few weeks later, the call came that he was gone. As you know, a few of us went to Istanbul, and finally after many hours of traveling and waiting in airports, we arrived. We went directly to the *tekke*, prayer lodge. There, Efendi lay in a wooden box at the feet of the tomb of Pir Nureddin Jerrahi. Just a few of us were present. The box was opened, and we saw him. This man whom I had known for so many years, who was so full of life and joy, was now motionless. His eyes were closed, and there was a hint of a smile at the edge of his mouth. Somehow we all felt physically smaller. We looked for a long time, then the box was closed.

That was on Thursday night.

Only two nights before, Efendi was at home enjoying an evening with his family. They ate and talked together. Later that night, about 2 A.M., when he went to make his late night prayers, he had trouble getting up from the floor. He called his wife, Baçi Sultan. She saw that something was wrong and telephoned her brother who lived down the street. Then she telephoned Sefer Baba, Efendi's first *khalifa*, deputy. Sefer Baba was himself sick that night. But he got dressed and made the trip through the winter cold to the sheikh's house.

After the calls, Baçi Sultan returned to the room. Efendi had great difficulty breathing. He gasped and intoned: *La ilaha illa Allah*, there is no god but Allah... three times, and then he was gone.

When his brother-in-law arrived, he tried to revive him. They placed a mirror to Efendi's mouth to see if he was still breathing. He wasn't. The doctor came and said that it was hopeless. Then Sefer Baba came and lay down next to him on the floor. Kemal Baba and Nedjdet Baba arrived, and they took the body back to the *tekke* in Karagumruk. There they washed him, prepared him, and put him in the box that we saw him in on Thursday.

The next morning at ten o'clock a few hundred people gathered in the *tekke*. We carried the coffin, a simple wooden box, from the old *tekke* into the yard and placed it beside Sheikh Fahreddin Efendi's window. After many prayers, dervishes lifted the box to their shoulders and carried it out through a little stone corridor into the street where it was snowing and cold. We walked down the small winding back ways of Istanbul. We each took turns carrying the box....

It must have taken half an hour to get to the Fatih Mosque. There we left Efendi outside, and all went in for Friday prayer. After prayer everyone in the mosque was told they could come out and say the special prayers for the dead. Somehow that crowd of a few hundred had swelled to thousands and filled the enormous courtyard adjacent to the mosque.

The dervishes lifted the box again and carried it through the small entranceway to the mosque. It was crowded, and there was almost no room to move. As if some giant wave were pushing us... we were moved forward. Many thousands followed the coffin back to the *tekke*. And as we looked ahead, we could only see the *taj*, the crown-turban resting on the coffin. It seemed as though Efendi was leading us. The police had blocked all the traffic from entering the route of the procession. People watched from windows and bridges. At the *tekke* bearers carried the coffin inside as riot police wearing large plastic face helmets stood guard to control the human flow. Anything might happen with so many people.

The night before, in the *tekke*, a grave was dug very close to where Fahreddin Efendi lies. Whoever could, crowded into that small corner. Dervishes took Efendi's body from the box and placed it in the earth, then covered it with dirt and planks of wood. Finally they poured cement over the wood. We all went to another part of the *tekke* to wait out the several hours it would take for the cement to dry. When it had dried we returned, placed the wooden sarcophagus on top of the cement, and folded cloths embroidered with the Name of Allah in gold over it. We placed Efendi's *taj* on the front end of the sarcophagus, and twenty of us did the ceremony of *dhikr*. For an hour, we stood there repeating the Name of Allah while standing on the grave of our spiritual teacher. . . .

Sefer Baba told me that for some reason, a short time ago, they opened one of the graves. It was the grave of Sheikh Yahya Moravi, who had died at the age of 120. He died in *halwat* and was placed in the earth sitting up, as he had died two hundred years ago. Sefer Baba said that his beard and his body were exactly as they were when they had placed him in the grave. There was no change. Sheikh Yahya sits next to Sheikh Muzaffer Efendi, right in that little corner of the *tekke*.

THE MAN OF MUD

 Allah said, "I was a hidden treasure, and I wished to be known, so I created man in order to be known." Within this statement, Allah reveals to us that man and nothing else on this planet has the capability and the capacity to know Him. And that it is Allah's wish for us to know Him. Within this statement is the entire essence and purpose of life.

Without this statement, it would require so much more of us to believe that it is possible to know Allah. Allah created the universe for man so man is the *macrocosm* or greater world while the universe is the *microcosm* or lesser world. Man is outwardly small but inwardly great. The universe was created outwardly great but is inwardly small. All that exists was brought into creation for the sake of man.

Allah created Adam, the first man. He created him out of water and earth. He kneaded this substance for a long time. The first part of the body of Adam that Allah allowed to become human was the head. So that Adam, the first man, could look from those eyes at his torso and limbs of mud, at his hands and fingers of mud, and realize that without Allah he was nothing more than a useless lump of clay. Without Allah, we are in a similar state. We can see through the eyes in our head, and we can think with this mind that Allah has given us, we can speak with this tongue and hear with these ears, but if this tongue does not repeat the Name of Allah, if this mind does not remember Allah, if these ears do not listen to hear the sounds of Allah's Name, if this body which has a means of even taking a shape of the Name of Allah does not do so, then we are as if blind and deaf, wandering around this planet, and we are really nothing more than a lump of clay that has some ability to move.

When the first man was complete, he was told to look over his right shoulder. There were three lights. He asked the first light its name and where it resided.

"I am Intelligence," it answered, "and I live in your head."

He asked the second light the same question.

"I am Conscience, and I reside in your eyes."

He looked at the third light and had to shield his eyes from the glow. "Who are you, and where do you live," he asked.

The light answered, "I am Compassion, and I live in your heart."

On the other side of the Prophet Adam stood three darknesses. He forced himself to ask the first darkness its name.

"I am Arrogance, and I live in your head."

"This is impossible," cried Adam, "for that is where Intelligence lives."

"Only until I enter; then there is no room for Intelligence," said the darkness.

"And who are you?" he asked, turning to the second darkness.

"My name is Insatiable Ambition, and I reside in your eyes."

"But that is where Conscience lives," replied Adam.

"Not when I am there," uttered Ambition.

"And you," he asked the third darkness, "who are you?"

"I am known as Envy, and I occupy space in your heart."

"Compassion is in my heart," said Adam.

"When I enter your heart," whispered Envy with a smile, "Compassion departs."

Islam is an inoculation against the ills, the pains, the diseases of the world. The greatest gift that Allah has given is the gift to worship Him. But He has also allowed us the free will to decide whether or not that is what we want to do. That decision is linked to everything about us, to whatever problems we may think we have in life, to whatever ills, to whether we're conscious about how we use our health before we lose it or how we use our leisure before we have none. It is all linked to an attitude that each of us has, whether we truly believe that Allah created man.

Al-Ghazali says that the drunken man has no idea about his drunkenness. He is drunk. The man who is not drunk, from the outside, is aware of the theory of drunkenness, but does not know what it's like to be drunk. The person who is outside of *Tassawuf*, Sufism, has a difficult time understanding the experience of what it's like to repeat the Name of Allah. The person outside of Submission to Allah, the person who may not have faith, is like a person looking at a drunken man. The one who's drunk with the Name of Allah can barely explain that experience to anyone else. And the person on the outside can find no way to understand it except as a theory. So experience in life is essential to give us wisdom. This kind of wisdom is not a wisdom that comes from books. It's not a wisdom that is something you can just pick up. It's a sacred knowledge that Allah has given as a gift to those who apply the knowledge they already have in their lives. If only the Truth could be unveiled as we unveil a statue and just look at it, and say yes, this is the Truth. Many have come before us and have told the Truth. Yet we cannot say that we understand the Truth, that we have within us the wisdom of the Truth. Because what is really important is not the Truth. What is important for each of us is our own personal discovery of the Truth. What our experiences are in making a discovery that allows us to have the Truth for ourselves. Otherwise the Prophet Muhammad gave it all to us; he told us the Truth. Allah sent a book and a man to give us an example, and yet we still live our lives with a certain number of veils that cover how and what we see.

We still have not understood that the manner in which we look at something will reveal untold bits of knowledge. We create blocks within our own lives and within our own experiences that do not allow us to see clearly. We will always agree with someone who tells us, "Well, you're right," or who will say the right thing. If we agree, then that person is correct. If we don't agree, then we put up a defense, and we block the possibility of knowing more.

How do we create these blocks for ourselves? What are they? One way that we always make a block that doesn't allow us to get closer to Allah is the misuse of our words. The heaviest burden that we can carry from one place to another is our words. As soon as we say something that criticizes someone, as soon as we say something that judges someone, this tongue which is locked behind two rows of hard teeth and two lips that close as soon as we allow words to go out without thinking first, and gossip or ridicule or say something about someone, we are creating a block that doesn't let us get close to Allah. That is why the Prophet of Islam said, "Hold your tongue," to somebody when he was asked, "What can I do to help myself?"

Because who a person is, is hidden beneath his tongue.

Why do we gossip? I think it's because we have a feeling that if we know something about something or someone that others don't, it gives us a certain power. It's a false understanding of power. But somehow, if we can say something about someone else to a third person who hasn't yet heard or known anything about it, it makes us feel important.

It's a false importance. It would be interesting for one week not to have to be right about every discussion we have. There are many instances in our daily life where we have a discussion, where we argue about something, and we may indeed be right. But it really doesn't matter one way or the other if we're right or wrong. It would be interesting, once in a while, to stop in the midst of an argument—on hearing someone else say something—and respond, "You know, I haven't looked at it from that angle. I'd like to think about it from your point of view, and let's talk about it another time."

Why do we think we are giving up something precious of ourselves if we do this? It's important to look at this, each of us, for ourselves, to let the other person win the discussion, even if we know we're right. I think one of the most detrimental parts of man, which keeps him separated from Allah, is gossip and his tongue and words that are misused.

This tongue that we use to pronounce the Name of Allah, and then to say to somebody, "you are stupid" or "I hate you," is absurd.

Sheikh Muzaffer used to tell the story about a sheikh who had a beautiful daughter. This daughter was coming to the age of marriage, and she had many suitors. She was so beautiful that handsome princes and rich men of position all wanted to win her hand in marriage.

Finally the sheikh said, "I'll ask three questions and give you three tasks. After you have completed these tasks, you will come back here. And the one who can succeed in all of them will be worthy of having my daughter's hand in marriage."

The next day they all gathered together, and the sheikh said, "I want each of you to go out and bring me the sweetest thing in the world."

The following day they all returned. Some brought honey, others the sweetest smelling flowers, or just anything that had the sweetest taste or aroma, anything sweet you could dream of that was on the planet, they brought. At the end of this long line was a poor, meek dervish of the sheikh.

The sheikh finally said to him, "What is it? Why are you here?"

He said, "Well, your daughter is very beautiful, and I am in love with her. And I would like also to attempt to answer these questions so that I may win her hand in marriage."

The sheikh said, "Well, all right." He could not stop what he had started.

The dervish was holding a box.

"What's in that box?" asked the sheikh.

He opened the box. Inside was the huge tongue of an ox.

The sheikh stepped back and said, "Is this some kind of a joke or a game you're playing with me, dervish? I asked for the sweetest thing in the world, and you bring me this tongue!"

The dervish said, "But, my sheikh, humbly I tell you that the tongue is the sweetest thing in the world, because the words that come from the tongue, if they are sweet words, they can make a sick person well. They can make an unhappy person happy. They can make someone who is sad and despondent feel that his life is worth living, and have joy. Surely, the tongue is the sweetest of all things."

The sheikh said, "All right, you win this one."

Then, addressing the others, he said, "The next thing you have to bring me is the most bitter thing in the world."

The next day, the suitors all came and lined up. They brought bitter herbs and all kinds of bitter-tasting foods, plants, and whatever it was that tasted really bitter and terrible. And there was Dervish Mehmet at the end of the line holding a box.

The sheikh said, "What is it now? What do you have to show us this time?"

Dervish Mehmet opened the box, and there was the same tongue.

Astonished, the sheikh said, "Surely you're playing a joke on us again. Yesterday you said that this was the sweetest of all things. Today you say it is the most bitter."

"My sheikh," Dervish Mehmet offered humbly and quietly, "if the tongue says bitter words, it can make a happy person sad. If the tongue says bitter things to someone, it can hurt his very heart. This tongue is so bitter it can even break a heart."

The sheikh reluctantly said, "All right, Dervish Mehmet, all right." He paused and then said, "And now, you come with me into the *tekke*."

They went into the *tekke*, went into his room in the rear, and the sheikh said, "Make me a coffee."

28

He had a metal container with tripod metal legs that stood on the floor. In it you placed coals from the wood that was burning in the stove. It was very hot and you could make coffee.

The sheikh, said, "Make me a coffee here."

Dervish Mehmet took some hot coals from the wood stove, and placed them in the container, and began to put coffee and sugar and water in the coffee pot. He moved the coffee pot back and forth over the hot coals, and soon the water began to boil. As it was bubbling, the sheikh said, "Now, dervish, tell me, what sound is this water making? What is it saying?"

Dervish Mehmet was at a loss. He really didn't know. He said, "I'm not sure."

The sheikh said, "Think about it, come back tomorrow, and tell me the meaning of the sound the water is making. And if you tell me this secret, you can have my daughter in marriage."

The dervish returned to his room upset, because he thought for sure there was no way he was going to know what this boiling water was saying as it bubbled in the coffee pot.

It seems that a friend of the daughter of the sheikh was cleaning up in the kitchen of the *tekke* and had overheard this conversation. She went to the sheikh's daughter and told her what had happened, word for word.

That night, when the sheikh returned to his quarters and sat in his chair, his daughter asked, "Dear Father, would you like a coffee before you go to bed?"

He said, "That's very nice of you. Thank you."

And so she began to make a coffee, and as she moved the pot back and forth over the hot coals, the water started to bubble. She glanced at her father casually and asked, "Oh, Father, tell me — it's an interesting sound this water makes when it's bubbling and making your coffee." She went on, "What can that mean? What does that sound say?"

He thought for a second and said, "All right," and he explained;

"The water is saying that I was a drop in a cloud. There was condensation and the cloud opened, and I came down to the earth as a drop of rain. As this drop of rain I landed on a seed. That seed grew into a tree. A woodsman came, and he cut part of that tree, and chopped it up for firewood. And then this firewood was placed in the stove, and the hot coals were taken and put into this container, and then this coffee was made, and so the water was saying—'What is burning me is from me.'"

The daughter didn't show any emotion. She said good night to her father, went directly to her room, and wrote down everything he had said, sealed it in an envelope, and gave it to a friend to deliver to Dervish Mehmet. Because, as he was in love with her, she was in love with him.

He received the letter, opened it, and was amazed to see that the sheikh's daughter herself had sent a note with the answer to the sheikh's question. The next day, he went to the sheikh's apartment in the *tekke* as he had been instructed to do the day before. The sheikh greeted him, *"As-salaam aleykum.* Make me a coffee."

His dervish answered, *"Wa-aleykum as-salaam,* my sheikh," and began to prepare the coffee. He moved the pot over the hot coals.

The sheikh looked at him and said, "Dervish, can you answer the question, what is this bubbling water saying?"

Dervish Mehmet reflected within himself very deeply, as if he was thinking hard, then he said, "Ah, my sheikh, *Bismillah,* my sheikh, this water is saying. . ." and he repeated exactly what was in the letter, exactly what the sheikh had said the night before. In conclusion, the dervish added, "And the water is saying, what is burning me is from me."

The sheikh's face turned red. He looked at him and said, "Ah, dervish, and what is burning *me* is from me."

One should watch one's tongue. Especially in daily life. And there's no question about the tongue being watched within the *tariqa,* the Sufi path. Because the tongue can truly be the sweetest or the most bitter thing in the world. How often have we had the experience of feeling fine, and then we look at somebody and say, "You are beautiful today," or "How kind it was of you to do that for that person," or "My heart really goes out to you." Observe how that person is affected. We've also had the experience of being grumpy, and we just look at someone and say, "Look, get out of here," or "I dislike you," and we know the effect that has without even taking it to a point of gossip. Within gossip, the soul of the speaker as well as that of the listener can be lost.

The tongue is tied to the heart. It is said that a man's character is hidden beneath his tongue, because the tongue says what is in the heart. So when we speak, we're expressing what is in our hearts. And though Allah says He cannot fit in the entire universe but can fit into the heart of a believer, He doesn't say that He will fit in that heart if it's cluttered with bad thoughts, deeds, and questions. Such a heart must first be clean.

The Prophet Adam was born yesterday. Every morning when we get up, we are born in that way again. When we open our eyes in the morning and we look at ourselves, it's as if Allah has created us right then and there. If we remember Allah while we are alive, Insha'Allah, God willing, at the moment of our death, He will allow us to remember Him. If, for example, you spend all of your time on baseball statistics, then that's what you'll be thinking about all the time. If you spend all of your time thinking of Allah, then that's where your attention will also be. The actions of the *murid*, disciple, affect the heart of the sheikh.

Hazrati Rabia performed many prayers, all the time. She was immersed in prayer, in *dhikr*, in remembrance. She did so many prayers that her feet were always swollen. The people around her said, "Hazrati Rabia, why? We know you are close to Allah, why do you have to continue to do so many extra prayers?"

And she said, "These *dhikrs*, these prayers that I do are for the sake of those servants of Allah who do not pray and remember Him."

This is what the true sheikh does. He doesn't reveal your true nature which he sees. Instead he does more work, more inner work, more prayer, more *tesbih*, for your benefit without your ever knowing it. We have no idea of the joy that we give our sheikh, or the pain. We're barely conscious of how we affect other people around us in our life, so how could we be conscious of how we affect someone of that quality?

The longer our life becomes, the more experiences we have, the more our life shortens. It's an interesting thought. As we have more and more experiences, our life is shortened at the same time. One would almost think that the more experiences we have, the more understanding we gain, that our life would expand. But the nature of life is that it lessens with every breath we take.

Previously we spoke about certain things we could do to help us see ourselves and our natures a little better. These are only suggestions. But we can never know whether something will be helpful unless we try it. It is from the action, from the activity, that wisdom will come.

If you see a painting of a beautiful field and a tree and a river with pretty flowers on its banks, you can look at that painting and say: "What a beautiful country scene this is." But it's your imagination saying this. Because the experience of that field, of those flowers, that river, belongs to the painter, the man who stood in the shadow of a tree protected from the sun in the field as he felt the wind and listened to the rush of the river. That was the experience. And that can't be the experience of someone looking at a canvas who allows his imagination to believe he was there by the river. It can't be as complete. It may inspire you to go to that place and have your own experience of the field, the flowers, and the river.

If we could really understand how to watch our words, to know that spoken words are like seeds that we plant which will eventually grow into something sweet or bitter. If you plant peppers, you can't expect sugarcane. Our actions in this life are seeds we're planting for the other life promised by Allah.

There have been enough people that we've known, read about, experienced in some way, to make us feel that the path to Allah is surely better than what the gloss of the world has to offer. A world which we know is only temporary. It's all rented, whatever it is. Either it will go before us, or someone takes it from us, or its life expectancy reaches completion or we grow out of it. Or we'll die before it does.

The only thing we'll be able to take with us are our good deeds. And the Prophet Muhammad said to follow each bad deed with a good deed. This will erase the bad deed. To do something like this, we have to be conscious of our actions. Because what might appear as not really a bad thing in the dialogue of the world could not necessarily be a good thing within the explanation of Allah. I mean we can have an argument with somebody and make them feel bad and think, "Well, that's life, that happens." If we give way to our anger and later put honey on the wound that we inflict we have to understand first that we may have used a part of our body in a way that has hurt someone. Because we use our body in many ways. We use it as a weapon as well as a tool. It's a place of pleasure, of pain, of happiness, of sadness.

And Allah has allowed us with this body to say His Name, hear His Name, think His Name, and form His Name, so that we can be closer to Him. When the Qadari dervishes sit in their *dhikr*, they sit cross-legged. Their fingers form the Name of Allah. Part of the body takes the shape of the Name of Allah.

How much closer can that message be given to us than the signs on our hands? That part of our body that begins every kind of work. That begins a greeting. That begins an embrace. That begins a way of taking food. There are messages everywhere.

There is an important ingredient called time which spans the distance and space between the seed and the fruit. And the tree that takes the longest to bear fruit is not the fig tree or the date tree. It is man. Man takes the longest to bear fruit. This shows that we should have patience with other people. We have to have patience with all people. As we need an *adab*, proper behavior, for ourselves, we need patience for ourselves. Within the name of Adam, in Arabic, Allah has left a secret of how to live: standing in prayer, bowing in prayer, prostrate before God.

Allah has left traces and messages everywhere, right now, today, in every one of our lives. The more veils we can lift, the more we can see with the eyes of our heart, allow for a deeper understanding.

Insha'Allah, God willing, we can use this body to perform the good things in this life. And these ears to hear the Name of Allah, and this tongue to say the Name of Allah.

For Allah has shown us that what He has put outside us is also inside us. There are oceans, great bodies of salt water, and the tears that we sometimes shed are salted. There are lakes with sweet water, and our saliva is sweet. There are rivers in which the water is bitter, and the fluid in our ears is bitter. So Allah shows us that we are a miracle connected to the miracle of the Universe. We are a universe unto ourselves.

So, *Insha'Allah*, as each day goes by, we shall lift these veils that block us.

THE HIDDEN GAME

When he awoke, he found himself in a place that was very dark. He tried to move and found that his body touched the sides of the walls. He couldn't remember ever arriving at this place. It was dark, like a narrow pit. His hands couldn't find an entranceway, and he couldn't see. It was dirty, and he was shackled at the waist. In the distance, he heard the Name of Allah repeated again and again. There was moisture, and he felt he was swimming or sometimes just floating. But he had no idea where he was, or how he got there. The walls were shiny. It wasn't a place that he chose to be. One day he just woke up in this prison and thought that's where he belonged, because there seemed to be no way out. Finally, after what seemed to be a long, long time—he had no measure of time—there was enormous movement and pushing, as if he were in an earthquake. He felt a terrible pain. He was being forced out of this dark, narrow, confined place. He resisted, because he had gained an undefined comfort in the area he had come to know. Prison or not, it was his space. He wasn't sure where he was being forced to, but the pressure continued. Finally, he was pushed out into the world, through the birth canal of awareness into the ocean of consciousness. Later, the cord that shackled him and fed him was cut, and he was released. The pain stopped, and years later he was to discover two other places in his body that could be cut and he would have no pain, his fingernails and his hair.

The food that nourished him now became different. He drank the milk of his mother and one day was weaned from that. He began to eat other foods. Because even mother's milk blocked him. This didn't allow him to have the possibilities, the tremendous possibilities of eating the kinds of foods which Allah had placed on the earth for man to eat and be nourished by.

So he was weaned from one food and began eating another food. As he grew, he seemed to move further away from where he had been before and had a sense of a dark place. He also sensed himself being separated from something that he in his heart loved, and he lost a certain taste for the nourishment of the world. At that moment he entered the hidden game.

The hidden game is the road back to Allah. It is the understanding of where we came from, where we are, and where we are going. All of life is a weaning process. We are weaned from the milk of our mother, we are weaned from the food of the earth until we are nourished by something else.

When he came out of that place, his body was incomplete. Through the years it would find a completion. It would grow and become strong and be nourished and become more perfect. At the same time that his body was growing, his heart was doing the same thing. For although his heart was like a little jewel, it was incomplete.

It's not this conical shaped pump that lies within our chest, but a subtle entity and essence that Al-Ghazalli calls the heart. That subtle entity takes in all impressions, is how we learn, understand, and gain knowledge. Anyone who taints or teaches bad things to the heart of a child, which is like a jewel, will one day have to answer to Allah. For it's the heart of a child that imitates the hearts of those around him. And there's an enormous responsibility to having a child near you. For that child is going to imitate not only your actions, but even the subtlety of your feelings. And that responsibility will be questioned one day.

How does this heart become nourished? How does it grow and come closer to perfection? And how is this accomplished in our daily life? Because that's where it has to be done. That's the learning ground.

Disobedience to Allah is an ailment. And obedience to Allah is a medicine. If a doctor writes a prescription for our body, which may be ailing, he will give it to us within a certain context and schedule and proportion. Within that prescription, if he's a good doctor, will be a secret as to how our bodies could be cured. How many spoonfuls you take, at what hours of the day, and how many times during the day, are all part of the cure. If you took all the medicine at once, you would become sicker than before, and it wouldn't cure you. So it is with the nourishment of the heart.

Dhikr Allah nourishes and satisfies hearts. The remembrance of Allah is a nourishment and a medicine for the heart. The sheikh is a doctor. The portions and sequence are important. How many times you repeat a particular Name of Allah, the time of day you repeat it, and also on what days. The days you repeat certain Names are a secret within the *tariqa*. I remember when Sheikh Sefer Efendi gave some of us certain Names to repeat as our medicine, he said, "You can mark this down, these Names on these days, but then memorize it and throw the paper away, because the secret is in what Names are said on certain days."

Allah has given us these things in proportion. Bowing is half of a prostration, and the morning prayer is half of the noon prayer. There's a message and a secret in that. The only way this can be revealed to us is through our activity in the process of our development and the practices that we perform each day. Only through our own prayers and with the help of a sheikh can we reach this understanding.

How can we tune in every day? How can we reach the awareness of the traces of Allah around us and not forget Him? There are two reasons for remembering Allah. One is because we have forgotten Him. Therefore we remember Him because we have forgotten Him. And there are those who remember Him all the time.

For them it is a terrible pain to have forgotten Allah for a moment. For us it is after long periods of time of forgetting Him that we remember Him.

But how to remember Him? Not just by walking down the street and remembering Allah and then going on as before. When we partake of food and say *Bismillah*, in that moment, we are putting the *Nur* of Allah, the Divine Light of Allah, into that food. And that food in turn nourishes us. Why is it nourishing us? Not to gain physical strength to dig ditches and build bridges. The true reason for food to nourish us is to acquire the strength to pray to Allah. To have the strength to worship Him.

If we are attracted to the worldly, there is a good chance that we will forget Him. If we can eliminate some of these worldly attractions from our own life, chances are very good that we will remember Him. We remember what is close to us. A person who loves to eat never forgets when it's time for a meal. And a person who loves to pray and remember Allah never forgets the time for prayer and remembering Allah. It all narrows down to what we really love in our life. How much attention we're willing to give to the world outside. What we can bring of our inner world to that outside world. Because we live with and are involved in others. Relationships are divided into four categories. You have a private relationship, one perhaps when you're standing before Allah, or when you sit at the edge of your bed at night, just that moment before you lie down, and you remember Him. It's a private relationship. Nobody knows about this. Then there's a personal relationship, one that you have with people who are close to you. Wives, husbands, family. There's a professional relationship, one you have with those people you see in your daily work. Some people have what could be termed a sociological relationship, a relationship with society in the sense that they don't even know whom they are touching. For example, a radio personality. He doesn't know if anyone's listening. You can turn him off or on whenever you want. But he is, in that moment, perhaps reaching millions of people. Someone who writes a book doesn't know who is reading that book.

There's a real obligation when one performs within the context of a sociological relationship. You do the best you can, hoping it comes from your heart, because you're influencing people whom you don't even know, you may never see or talk to. That's a responsibility.

When I look at all this in a relationship, I ask myself why? Since my private relationship with Allah is the most special in my life, why do I spend the least amount of time in that relationship? And although I may invite some people from my professional relationship into my personal one, or even on a rare occasion invite someone from my personal relationship into my private one, why is it that the relationship that is the most important is also the one I spend the least amount of time in? And the one that is the least important, this professional relationship, seems to take up all of my time. So when I think of my life and how I spend my time, I look at this breakdown. Perhaps I can take an inventory and see what are the things I can do in my life to adjust the situation. For if I really believe that the private relationship to Allah is the most important one, and ultimately it does affect all my other relationships, why can't I find the time to be with it more? I'll miss a prayer, but I'll never miss lunch. I won't make my *tesbih* one day, but I'll make sure to have coffee every morning.

Then I look at myself, and I try to see who this person is whose heart goes out in a certain way but whose body and mind don't always follow. Part of that is because the heart has not been perfected as yet. So when I realize that my heart has not been perfected, that it needs more work, then I try to see how I can accomplish this. Because I know—I know when I feel good and when I feel bad. I know that I feel good when I'm in *dhikr Allah*. Every part of my body knows. And I know that I feel bad when I overeat,

39

when I'm angry or filled with tension. So I've examined this, and when I'm certain as to what things make me feel good and alive and a part of this world, then I can start to take an inventory and see what can be discarded from my life so that I can make room for something else that I know and feel is better.

Now it's not so easy to take inventory when the shop is open. Because the shop is full of customers walking around, trying to buy things and wanting to know about sales or bargains. So I decide that the best thing to do is to close up shop for a few days. I'll turn off my telephone, I'll stock enough food for a few days, and I'll tell all of my friends that I'm going out of town for the weekend. I won't turn on the TV, and I won't turn on the radio or record player. I will be there, in my room, with the things that are familiar to me. I will begin to get a picture of myself in that situation. Am I fidgety? Do I want to listen to music? Do I say, Well, okay, I'll play a *dhikr* tape? And use that as an excuse? How can I find out whether I really can be alone by myself? This is what a dervish retreat is. Because before one can be with Allah, one has to know how to be with oneself. Fahreddin Efendi describes the dervish retreat as a place that, for the first twenty-four hours, you would do anything to escape. Anything at all. But after the first day, you've moved from the consciousness of the Pharaoh to the consciousness of Moses. And at that point, you will do anything to stay there.

I ask all these things because I wonder what do we really do after we have been pushed out of that painful dark pit into this world that Allah has created for man. Allah said, I've created man for myself, I've created the entire universe for man.

How can we appreciate this universe unless we begin to explore it? And between that point of birth and another that will surely come to each of us, our death, there is a period of time that is unique. No one knows how long this time will last. We call it life. I wonder if we have the right to call it life. Do we live that life? Do we explore that life? Only those who really live that life, truly in every moment, can call it life.

But if we wander around in a semisleep, with veils over our eyes, and we neither see nor experience anything of Allah, where we've forgotten Him more than we remember Him, how can we call that life? Because whatever it is, one day it will end so abruptly that it will be frightening. And the only way it won't be frightening is if we are ready to live life with the understanding that It is a gift of Allah. A gift that we have no right to refuse. And by not living it, we are refusing it by not acknowledging it. We barely say thank you. Sometimes we don't even want to say thank you.

I'm really interested in how to get out of that state. Because each of us at one time or another has experienced it. How to remove these veils. How to live this life. To accept this gift, to be thankful to the Giver, to know where we came from and where we are and where we are going and to have love and fear of Allah. Very poor people in the ghettos say: "No hope, no fear." It's true. When there's no hope, there's no fear. And then you're capable of doing anything. Hope comes from Allah. Faith in Allah is a cloak, one that will always be too large for us. One that will never shrink although we could possibly grow into it.

When one loves Allah, one fears Him. Not that one fears the punishment of Allah, but one fears that Allah may decide not to call you his servant, may not return your love and push you far from Him for some reason. Fear that we could get so close and make a mistake. It's the fear that even for a moment we are not near Him.

A man approached Moses and said to him, "You are going to the mountain to speak to Allah. I have sinned my whole life. Ask him if I will be forgiven or punished."

Some time later, Moses came down from the mountain.

The man said, "Did you ask Him?"

Moses said, "Yes, I asked Him."

"What did Allah say?"

"Allah said, 'Tell my servant—'"

The man interrupted, "Stop! I don't care if Allah sends me to hell or punishes me with the greatest punishment on earth. But He has called me His servant, and if He thinks of me as His servant, then surely I am close to Him."

We desire beauty in our lives. We want to fill our lives with beauty. Yet how beautiful are we? How kind are we to others? Others whom Allah has also created. Do we ignore the Creation of the Creator? We say we love Allah, but we behave as if we don't love His Creation. Do we thank Him for putting tiny lenses in our head so that we can see for miles? He's given us a mind, and do we remember Him with this mind? He's put a little flesh in our ear that can hear sound. Are we thankful for that? And this tongue, this piece of flesh in our mouth, do we use it to pronounce His Name?

We forget. Life takes hold of us like a magnet. Pulls us, until we forget why we are really here. How do we dissolve that attraction, how do we find some solution that will allow us to be free of the desires of the world, but still enable us to live in it? How do we become a hinge, like a hinge on a door that opens into two different worlds and makes it one? How to become a hinge between our inner and outer life? How to become this pivot point that can move back and forth with a kind of ease and trust so that we don't get trapped in that outside world?

To become that hinge and to explore this life is a gift. To worship Allah and to remember Him, to realize that everything is invisible except that which we make semivisible. With awareness we can make all things visible.

If everyone closed his eyes in this moment, all the myriad objects in a room and all the books, pictures, and keepsakes wouldn't exist. When you go from your house and come to my house, you leave your house. It is no longer necessary to take your house with you. You can be here. And when you leave here and go to your house, you can leave here. Whatever is here is no longer necessary. If we can have things from the outside world and look at them in that way, then we can use them correctly. Whatever they are. When I leave here and go to my friend's house, I don't have to take my carpets with me. It's not necessary. If I take my car and go to another friend's house, I need my car to travel through space in order to get to that place. But when I come to his house, I leave my car and go inside. I don't have to think, I need to carry my car with me.

It's all this extra luggage that we carry around in our minds that becomes a block for us. These are some of the veils that don't allow us to see clearly. Because when each of us was pushed through that birth canal, we came with nothing. They had to find a cloth to wrap around us. And that's how we will go, even those people for whom kingdoms are not enough space, they'll be satisfied with six feet of earth. They'll have no choice. The only thing that we can take with us is our good deeds.

There was a man who was a woodcutter. He heard that in the next village there were people who worshiped a gum tree. And he thought, I'm going to take my ax and cut down that tree. So he put his ax on his shoulder and walked down the path toward the town with the intention of chopping down that tree. He knew that Allah is One. And they were wrong to worship that tree. Before he approached the town, a figure jumped before him and announced that he was the Devil and asked, "Where are you going?"

The woodcutter answered, "I'm going to chop down the gum tree in the next village because the people there worship it."

The Devil told him, "Look, it's not necessary. Let them do what they do. You go and do what you want to do."

He said, "No, I insist. I have every intention to go."

The Devil tried to stop him. The man punched him down and jumped on top of him and held him there. Presently the Devil looked up at him and said, "Look, you've got me pinned down now. Let's make a deal. I will give you one piece of gold every single day. It will be under your pillow in the morning for the rest of your life if only you forget this task and go back home."

The man thought, Every day of my life?

The Devil said, "Yes. That's a promise."

He asked the Devil, "How do I know you'll keep this promise?"

"The first day that you don't find the gold, you can just take your ax, and come and chop down this tree."

He thought that seemed logical and agreed.

That night he had a sleepless night wondering whether the gold would be under his pillow or not. When he awoke in the morning, there was a piece of gold. He had visions of being an extremely wealthy man. Because he thought every day one piece of gold would appear. The next night, the anticipation of the gold again prevented him from sleeping well. And when he awoke, he searched under his pillow, and there was no gold. There was nothing. He looked all around, thinking that it might have fallen down, but it wasn't anywhere to be found. He got very angry, picked up his ax and said, I'm going to chop that tree into bits. And he stalked off to the village. At the same spot he met the Devil again.

He said, "You tricked me. So now I'm going to chop that tree down."

The Devil said, "Now look, let the villagers do what they want, and you go and you do. . ."

He said, "Never mind, I'm going to chop that tree down. Get out of my way."

And in a flash, this time the Devil was on top of him. He was weakened. As strong as he was, he couldn't move.

He looked up, and the Devil said to him, "Now do you want to know why it was so easy for me to overthrow you this time? Whereas yesterday, you threw me down, and were more powerful than I was."

He said, "Yes."

And the Devil said to him, "Yesterday you were going to chop the tree down because of your faith in Allah. And today you were going to chop the tree down because you didn't get the gold. If you desire gold, it will weaken you in this world."

We think gold will give us strength and power, but how it is used when we get it is really important. Not so much whether we have it or don't have it. But if it comes to us, if Allah wants it for us, then we have to consider where it comes from. And how to use it. If we spend all of our waking hours in this professional relationship of ours just to grab a few pieces of gold, we will lose, because it will take away from the time and energy we have for our most important relationship, and our hearts will not be nourished.

If Allah wants us to have that kind of gold He will create conditions for us to have it that will be far easier than any we can dream of. If He doesn't want us to have it, He will not create those conditions. And then we must know that it's enough just to do a hard day's work in order to make an honest living so that we can have the time and the place and the energy to nourish our hearts.

Ramadan is the Islamic month of fasting. One month of fasting. If all we do is not eat, then our only benefit is that we'll be hungry. There are many secrets to Ramadan. Each time we do this fast, some secrets may be revealed to us.

Fasting is the only worship of Allah done in total secrecy. Only Allah knows. It is said that when you fast, you should rub oil on your beard so others don't know you're fasting. We pray openly in front of other people, it is seen. When we give charity, we give it out. But fasting is a secret between each person and Allah. And only Allah knows whether you do it or don't do it. You can stay home and eat three meals a day and tell people you're fasting. Nobody knows. Allah knows. And you know.

But fasting from food is just a small part of Ramadan. We have to fast from our anger. We have to fast from being greedy, being unkind, being unfriendly. We have to have a fast of speech. Only say things that we really mean. Only hear those things that are necessary for us to hear. Only walk to those places that are necessary to go. No frivolity. And think that when we don't eat there are

45

people who, unlike us, cannot eat because there's no food.

And so we fast, and we take no food or water during the daylight hours. But in late afternoon our mind tells us: "Don't worry. Take a nap. You'll wake up in three hours. It will only be thirty more minutes, then you can eat."

There are people, as in Ethiopia, who have no food. They get down on their knees and follow an ant until that ant goes to its little hill where it has placed a seed, and they take that seed and eat it. We don't know about hunger. We take a hot shower every morning. There are people who have never had hot water.

So how do I explore this life? Maybe I take a hot shower. All right, it's there for me to use. Perhaps just before I step out of the shower, I make it very cold. And in that moment I know that there are people who don't have hot water. How many times have we given clothing to someone who was cold? A coat to a shivering man? A piece of bread to someone who's hungry? We don't stop to reflect that Allah has created everyone. We are not hungry like that man who had to follow an ant to get a seed.

Think, think about how you will make your next Ramadan. And like anything that's worth something, prepare for it. Let us not think only of ourselves.

It's difficult. We will get angry. There's tension. We're still working at our jobs. In this country it's required of us to continue doing everything we normally do. No one out there cares if you're eating or fasting. The boss doesn't care. He wants the job done. Ramadan is the most wonderful opportunity to see oneself. How short we are with someone else if we're hungry. Just a little hungry. What's our temper like? Do we get angry? Can we not get angry? And after we've taken that first bit of food during the *iftar*, break of fast, do we forget the rest of the day? And then do we just have this big feast? That's not it. We are not talking about having a feast every night.

Allah comes very close to the believers during Ramadan. He gives us the most wonderful opportunity to see who we are and how we are. How we are toward ourselves and how we are toward others. So that we can use this in our daily life.

I suggest that all of us really think about Ramadan. Read the *hadith*. Talk to people. Get a measure of how we will spend the month of fasting. Then do it, use it as a laboratory.

There is a charity for everything. The charity for the body is fasting. After we've gone a whole month not having cigarettes, maybe we don't have to pick them up again. We like to have adventures, so we do things that obviously endanger our health. The packet says so. We read it every day. Is smoking adventure, defiance, or a wish for oblivion?

Insha'Allah, we will think about these things. And that Allah will give us each a good Ramadan. One in which we can learn. And to carry it through, not just to leave it after it's finished. But to use it as a teacher. And to be appreciative that Allah has given us so much, that we are truly the wealthiest people in the world. The fact that Allah lets us swallow our food—isn't that a gift? If you could not swallow your food, if you had to throw up and vomit your food, would it make any difference if you vomited into a solid gold bowl? None.

We are extremely wealthy, wealthier than millionaires. Yet we take our riches for granted. As if they are due. So, *Insha'Allah*, we can be thankful and use these ears to hear the Name of Allah. And these eyes to see the traces of Allah everywhere. And this tongue to say the Name of Allah. And this wonderful mind to remember Allah.

THE COAT

The path of Sufism is not one of total seclusion. Where we practice what we've learned in seclusion is in the world. A friend told a story a little while ago about some men who went to a restaurant, divided all of their food, and left a portion for the poor children to eat. This reminded me of an incident that occurred in Konya, in central Turkey. I had some conversations with Qadari and Rufai sheikhs. These conversations took place in a little shop close to the Mevlana Museum. It was during Ramadan. The shopkeeper, Ahmet, came onto the street afterward and asked if I would come and have *iftar*, break of fast, with him in a restaurant across the street. I thanked him, accepted his invitation, and at the right time went there to break my fast. As I sat in the restaurant, he was walking around serving other people, opening the door and talking, and I realized that he must be the owner of this restaurant. He prepared a meal, brought it to me, and sat down next to me. I asked him, "Is this also your restaurant? The shop down the street, and this restaurant?"

"Indeed," he said, "Allah has given me this gift of having two shops."

A traveler came to the door of the small restaurant. He had a huge sack, which he put down. He was dusty from being on the road. He said, "As-salaam aleykum," and was answered with "Wa aleykum as-salaam." Ahmet brought him in and sat him down.

The traveler said, "Excuse me, but I have no money."

Ahmet said, "Oh, sit, sit down, please."

He sat him down at a table just like everyone else and brought him a fine meal. When the man finished, Ahmet gave him a glass of tea. When he finished his tea, the man got up and put his sack on his shoulder. Ahmet ran to open the door. He held the door open and said, "*As-salaam aleykum*, please come back."

I noticed this happened with two or three people during the course of the evening. They didn't pay for their meal, obviously because they didn't have money, yet it was a joy for Ahmet to serve them. Besides just serving them the food, there was a very important thing that he did, which I feel is critical to understanding what mankind can be. He treated them with enormous respect, and not once did he lessen their dignity.

This is real Islam. Within Islam no one takes your dignity away. This is an extremely important thing to man. And it is one of the reasons that the people of the West don't understand the people of North Africa and the East. Africa is beyond them and they can't understand the Asian mind. Partly because Westerners still feel that Asia is about the size of Europe, and don't realize that in fact five Europes can fit into Asia.

Besides that, they don't understand that a simple man, regardless of his profession, as long as it's an honest means of earning his living, carries within him the dignity of a king. Which is not the same here. We place our parents in old-age homes and think their experiences in life cannot teach us. How smug we are. Consciously or unconsciously, we strip the dignity from those who we believe are less than us.

The dervish considers another person before himself. He sees the good in a person, and acknowledges that good.

It's important in this life to retain our dignity and not to let anyone take it from us. The cloak of Islam, the cloak of faith, preserves that dignity within each of us. Allah created us, how can we not have dignity? How can we, as long as we believe that Allah did indeed create us, ever thank Him enough? How can we ever thank Him for these eyes? For this heart? It's not even so much how we can thank Him. But do we really want to thank Him? If we really do want to thank Him, why don't we? What is that strange element in man's nature which covers up the feeling of being created by Allah? Which covers up a moment of seeing how to thank him? Allah asks Man the following:

—O son of man, why did you not visit me?

—But, Allah, where could I visit You? You are Allah, Lord of the Worlds.

—One of my servants was ill. If you had visited him, you would have found Me with him. I asked you for food, and you did not feed me.

—Allah! how should I feed You?

—You walked past somebody on the street who asked you for food . . . he was hungry. If you had fed him, then it would be as a reward from Me. I asked you to give to drink, and you did not give Me to drink.

—But Allah, how should I give You to drink when You are the Lord of the Worlds?

—You passed My servant on the road who was thirsty and you didn't give him water. If you had, you would have gained My reward.

At moments like that, we intellectualize. And we miss the moment.

We think, that man is a drunkard. Why should I give him a few pennies? He says he wants bread, but *I* know he'll go and drink alcohol. This is how we reason, and then we make excuses for not giving him those few pennies. Because in that moment we've intellectualized it.

Dhul Nun was praying by the river. When he had finished his prayer, he looked down and saw a scorpion. The scorpion began to move, and Dhul Nun followed the scorpion. Like the wind, the scorpion went across the river to the other bank. There under a tree a man was sleeping. Dhul Nun saw that a snake was just near the man and was going to bite him. The scorpion ran up the tree, came straight down, and killed the snake. Then, like the wind, went over to the other side of the river again.

Dhul Nun followed, and he said, with his arms open, "Ya, Allah, this man must be such a good man. He must love You so much that You would send one of Your vast army to protect him."

And a Voice came to him, a Voice that had no sound and made no words said: "This man was a drunkard. That's why he was sleeping in the daytime. But am I not the Lord of all creatures? Am I not the Lord of all men?"

All of what we see outside ourselves is a lesson if we can learn to see with the eyes of our heart. Everything we see when we sit quietly and meditate on Allah is a lesson. If we see a person who's blind, it's a lesson to us to be thankful to Allah that we have these eyes. When was the last time that any of us thanked Allah for these precious eyes? We don't even think to thank Him for that, and yet if we see somebody blind, something in us is touched. At that moment, our heart sinks, and we can say Ya, Allah, thank You, Allah, for these eyes.

We were created from nothing, from a little drop of water. A drop of water that contains all of our intelligence, all of our bones, skin and muscles and everything that we are. And when we drink tea or a glass of water, it goes through 302 different sieves to get to our stomach. So everything on the outside, if we look at it in the right way, can be a lesson for us to remember who we are.

It's not necessary to look for miracles outside ourselves. But to learn how to submit and to accept. These are really the things that each of us must become aware of in our daily life. Because it's different for each of us. Our days are different. How do we use what is presented to us when we work so hard and at the end of the day we look and say, "How did it get to be so late? This day has flown by." And what have we done for Allah during that day?

I think we have to examine our lives. How we get up in the morning. How we spend our time. What we do, how much we remember Allah. How much we even remember ourselves. Here is a human being created by Allah, moving through space. What beauty! What a miracle! This incredible factory, which you can put food and water into, digests and goes through all kinds of machinations to come out and purify you.

There is a *hadith*. The Prophet said, Consider your health before you may become ill, your prosperity before you may become poor, your age before you become old, your leisure before you have none.

Now two out of those four were said as a probability. Consider your prosperity before you *may* become poor. It doesn't mean that you will. But you may. You must consider your health before you *may* become ill. But the two things that *will* happen are these: We *will* get old, and the day *will* come when we will no longer have any leisure.

Now how do we look at that? Do we just say: What an interesting saying. It sounds good. I agree with that. And then let it go.

The *hadith* are examples of how to behave as a human being in this life. How do we look at behavior and humanness, examining what they mean to each of us? What does it mean to consider your health before you may become ill? When you look at that statement, does it mean how do you treat yourself? Do you understand that we have a body, and that we put food in this body? Do we take care of it? No matter how wealthy we are, we cannot replace every part of the body. And no matter how poor we are, we can never find a way to obtain anything that's more valuable than our health. How do we consider this every day?

How do we consider our prosperity before the possibility comes that we have none? That we are poor? What does this mean to us? Do we not think we are prosperous? Do we only think people who are millionaires are prosperous? Are we not prosperous if we have enough to pay our rent and buy good food to eat every day? To have a clean house? Isn't that a prosperity? To have clean clothes? A corner to pray in?

How do we think about all this? Of our age? Do we think about our youth before we become old? We have examples all around us.

COAT

Our parents, grandparents, they may not even be alive anymore. Great-grandparents probably are not. Friends, uncles, aunts, relatives—gone! Or old. Are they not examples for us? How much time do we really think we have? The most precious thing we have is our breath. Each breath. Each single breath. That's how we measure our life. Because when you look back over the last twenty or thirty or forty years, it's like the snap of a finger. You look back, it's a second. A blink of the eye.

When you think of it, even if you wanted to think of all the things that you can remember in your life up until this moment, it wouldn't take you very long. It certainly wouldn't take you the thirty or forty years that you took to live it! Why do we think the next twenty or thirty or forty years will be any different? They won't. Unless we introduce love into our life. Unless we introduce a love for mankind into our life.

How can we love Allah, how can we say we love Allah and not love that which He has created? This is absurd. If we truly want to love Allah, if we have any notion that we want to love Allah, we must love Him through His Creation. That's His expression of Himself to us.

If two people are in love, and you put them in a room overnight, and in the next room you put a man with a toothache, in the morning the lovers will come out and say that the night flew by. It was like a minute. Where did that night go to? The man with the toothache will say that it was the longest night of his life. He thought it would never end.

There is a difference within us. We've each experienced life differently through whatever means, our prayer, our *tesbih*, our meditation of Allah. Our way of glimpsing the traces of Allah, which He has left for us to see and to learn from, is a knowledge that in those moments, in those times in our lives, we are better than when we are veiled.

Yet it still isn't enough. We don't understand submission. There

54

was a sign in the *tekke* in Istanbul, a calligraphy that I saw years ago. I looked at it, and I didn't know what it said. Underneath the main letters were two red drops, and I asked someone their meaning. They said, "Ya, Shems, this says *Ah Tesslimiyet*. Oh, this submission to Allah is so difficult that you can cry tears of blood."

It's not just difficult for us. It's difficult because in this world man has chosen the way of other men, not the way of Allah.

There was a sheikh, a great sheikh in Istanbul, and he had a *murid*. And this *murid* of his inherited an enormous fortune from his uncle. It was a legitimate inheritance. He went to his sheikh and said, "My sheikh, this is what happened. My uncle passed away and left me this money." It was a sum equivalent to a million dollars. He asked, "What should I do?"

The sheikh said, "If you want the things of this world, take the money. But if you don't want the things of this world, then leave it."

The *murid* said, "My sheikh, what I want to do is just to be near you."

The sheikh said, "Then give all the money away, every penny."

He went into the streets and started to give this money away. It was not an easy task. It was a lot of money. And he went to all the poor neighborhoods and knocked on the doors, and he gave away money, and everywhere he went he brought bread and food for everyone. He went to the mosque and gave the *imam* an enormous sum of money so that he could rebuild the mosque, which was falling down. After some weeks, he finally managed to give all the money away. Every last cent.

On his way back to see his sheikh, the *imam* ran after him in the street and said, "You've done so much for everybody. Here, take this. You're wearing such a threadbare coat. I bought you a new coat. It's a gift for you."

He didn't really want the coat, but he felt that it was a gift, and he couldn't refuse, so he took it. He arrived at his sheikh's wearing this new coat. The sheikh asked if he had given all of the money away. And he said, "Yes, every cent of it."

He asked, "Then where did you get this coat?"

He told him the story, that the *imam* had given him this coat as a gift for giving so much to the mosque.

The sheikh said, "Well, if you like this coat so much, I'll see that you wear it—always. I'll see that you wear it in this life, and I'll see that you wear it also in the next life."

He took the coat, and he threw it on the street. He had ordered a dozen *lachmajun*, a kind of pizza, and threw them all on the coat. All of the neighborhood dogs came running over and started eating, ripping the coat, and the sauce covered the lining. It became an old coat in a short time.

Then the sheikh said, "Now you wear this coat." He put it on. The sheikh said, "Come with me, we're going to visit a friend of mine, a Bektashi sheikh."

And they went to visit this Bektashi sheikh, and he said, "You wait outside for me. Now take off your hat."

He took his hat off and his long hair fell to his shoulders. The sheikh tied his hair onto a branch of a tree and left him hanging there. Then he said, "You wait here for me," and he went inside to visit his friend.

As they were having tea, the other sheikh felt uncomfortable. He could see through the window that this dervish was hanging from the tree by his hair.

The sheikh asked, "What's wrong? Do you feel uncomfortable?"

His friend answered, "Well, I wish you could do something about this dervish. It's upsetting me to see him like that."

He said, "You want him here? I'll call him." And he called this dervish by name to come to him. Hearing his name being called, the dervish pulled himself from the tree, ripping his hair and part of his scalp, and ran to his sheikh. His head was bleeding. The sheikh put his hand over the wound and healed him.

The other sheikh said, "I would like to have a little bit of the hair to hang on the wall of this *tekke*, so that everybody here can see what it is to be a real dervish."

And the sheikh gave it to him.

They then went to visit another sheikh. This time the sheikh took his dervish and put a nail through his ear lobe into the door of the house, and left him hanging there. And he said, "You wait here for me."

The sheikh went in, and began talking to his friend. They had tea. And this friend was also very uncomfortable seeing this treatment.

So the sheikh asked, "You want him in?" and he called his dervish, who pulled himself from the door and ripped his ear off. The sheikh placed his hand over his wound, said *Bismillah*, and it was healed.

It is said that this dervish became a great sheikh. He wore the coat his entire life. And if you look in the section of the *tekke* in Istanbul, way in the back, the coat is draped over one of the sarcophagi. He wore that coat forever.

The submission to Allah is so difficult you can cry tears of blood. This is a true story. Nobody asks us to submit in this way. I'm not making it up to make a point. This actually happened. One can ask why did it happen? Isn't this extreme? Did it have to be that way? Whatever the case, whatever lesson that man had to learn was between him and his sheikh. It's not for us to question it or look at it in another way from the outside.

Yet we can learn from it. We can learn from it because our sheikh says one little thing to us, and we think, Oh, I don't know if I should do that. He asks one little thing, and we think, I don't know if there's time to do that.

For the dervish there are three conditions that are necessary for us to understand. The first is respect for ourselves. Next, respect for the society we live in. Then, we can have respect for Allah. If these three things are done correctly in that order, a person can become a "perfect man." But we can't skip. We can't say forget about me, and go to Allah. Nor can we say I want to forget about society, I want to forget about mankind, I just want to love Allah. Because when we say that, we are going against the understanding of Allah. There was a man from Kaysari, in eastern Turkey. I heard this in Madinah. He was a shoemaker. Everyone heard that Allah loved him. The scholars came and asked, "What's going on here? What are you telling people? How can you speak like this, that Allah loves you?"

He looked at them and he said, "Don't you love that which you create?"

Look how much we care for a little drawing or a piece of pottery if we make it. Or if we make a bench with some wood or a chair—look how much we care for that. We put something of ourselves in it. We're connected to it. So if Allah has created each of us, it's a miracle, really. Surely He didn't create us to abandon us. He gave us the means and the capacity to be close to Him. But He left it for us to do what's necessary to get there.

This has to do with each of us in our own lives. *Sacred knowledge is a Bride who comes to the door.* Like a miracle. And when She comes to a door and opens it and sees that the one inside is not prepared, She goes back to Her Father. If we want to have a relationship with sacred knowledge, an intimate relationship, and we want sacred knowledge to come and enter our house, we first have to clean our house. Or else this Bride will come to the door and see that this house is not ready, and go back to Her Father.

I would ask what have we done, each of us, in the last week? We gather, we talk together. We talk about real things to do. This is not theory. We have to act and take responsibility for our actions. Whatever they are. But if we do a bad deed, know that we have to follow it with a good deed. And know that a good deed can erase a bad deed.

In order to do that, we have to be tuned into what is acceptable and what is not. It doesn't mean that we'll stop doing it. Only Allah knows. He knows what we are capable of.

58

What I would like to do is to suggest that each of us take a *hadith* and in the next week really see how it applies in our life. See what it means to us. How long will we go on not recognizing the messages that Allah has placed on our bodies? Whether they be through the gray hairs, or the wrinkles, the tiredness, whatever. These are all messages. How long do we think we will stay young and healthy? How long do we think that we'll have such leisure that we can do anything we want? Just hang around, drink a lot of coffee. How long before we rip the veils from in front of us? Rip them and burn them, so they cannot come back.

This is really what's important. A basic, very basic going back to ABC. Someone came to the Prophet Muhammad and said, "Please, give me some help," he said, "and make it brief." The Prophet answered, "When you stand up in prayer, pray as if it's the last prayer you'll ever make."

When you stand up to pray, pray as if it's your last prayer. Do not say anything that you will have to apologize for later. These two things I think we could also do. We could take this as a private task. Because it may indeed be your last prayer. And if it isn't, are we thankful that it isn't? For one day, in the next week, for one day, morning until night, can we avoid saying anything to anyone that we would have to apologize for the next day?

Just to read the *hadith*, and to think how interesting and beautiful, what a wonderful saying, is not helpful. What's helpful is to take it and work with it. To take any *hadith* that you choose, continually, every day, every week, just take one, one a day, one a week, and see.

A SMALL CIRCLE OF LISTENERS

 *El medet,* to take refuge in, to ask for the help of the Masters who have come before.

We have to learn from those who have preceded us.

Kum kum ya habibi kan tanam, awake, awake my beloved, how you sleep. This is the state of man. We're in a condition of semisleep. Everyone here should consider this: all who have ever come to this planet have had to leave it. This will also be our lot. There are those who sat in my old house for years and years before me, and now they're gone. There will be those who sit here after me, and they also will be gone. There are those who lived in our apartments before us, and they're no longer there. Now it's ours, and another time it will be someone else's.

Life as we know it will end. The question is, can we grow past the point of decay? Faith in Allah is an inoculation against the pain and disease of the world. Faith in Allah is a protective cloak. I'm saying Allah. You can use the term God, Gott, Dios, whatever, as long as you mean the One God who has no partners.

Faith in Allah is a gift. As we can see, in the world around us, not everyone realizes that this gift is available nor do they accept it. Everything in the world is a gift from Allah. Everything good is a gift from Allah, and everything bad is the misuse of that gift.

The life Allah gave us should be measured in breaths, not in years. Because from infancy to old age, we learn, and we mature. We believe that as we grow older we have more understanding. This is not necessarily so. If one can understand that with every breath, our life is lessened, then our life acquires an immediacy.

Allah has created man so that he can live without changing his skin or his hair whether he is at the North Pole or in the desert. No other being is capable of this. If you take a polar bear and put him on the equator, or take a camel and put him at the North Pole, it will die. But man, by merely changing his outer clothes, can adapt and live anyplace on the planet. And by putting on certain clothes can even live in outer space.

If you take a herbivorous animal and you reduce the amount of plants that he can eat and eventually eliminate those plants, that animal will die. Yet man can cultivate the land and adapt to the existing food.

We all live together at the same time on the same planet and all have the same problems whether we are rich or poor. We can laugh today and be sad tomorrow. One day tender hands caress and soothe our head, while on another day we may have a headache. All of life is a weaning process.

This is from Mevlana Jelaluddin Rumi. The infant must be weaned from the breast that at one time gave it its complete nourishment. Then at another time it becomes a barrier to the hundreds of different tastes of food. So the child must be weaned. We must wean ourselves little by little. Wean those things out of our life that are no longer useful. That have become meaningless. That have become like toys in our life.

In each stage of our life there are things that may be good, but we must let go of them in order to gain and benefit from new foods that wait to nourish us.

As an embryo, our nourishment was blood. Then it became milk, and then we took solid food. At the point that we wean ourselves from solid food, we become interested in the hidden game. For us, the hidden game is Sufism.

There are many aspects of Sufism. Whether it be prayer, wearing particular clothes, the meaning of those clothes, telling beads.

But the most important thing about Sufism is helping others.

If anyone were to say to the embryo in the womb: "Look, you're living in this dark narrow pit, and outside is a beautiful world. Outside there's a sky that's not held up by any pillars and a carpet of earth beneath it that grows foods and plants and flowers and all kinds of edible things. There are trees and great beauty here. There are mountains and plains and fragrant fields. There are gardens and a sky with a hundred stars. Why don't you leave this place where all you're doing is drinking blood and sitting in this dark, confined and narrow space. Why do you linger in this darkness?"

Because of the state of the embryo, not having seen any of what was being described, he would be incredulous. He would feel that there's disbelief and deceit woven into the words.

The messengers of God have come, the great sheikhs have come, and they all told us of a beautiful world filled with pleasure and delight. That a whole other world than the one we know, where we go through so much pain and sorrow with only flashes of joy, exists. But we are like that embryo, lingering in the darkness of a confined, narrow space.

There have been those that have come to tell us and teach us this, and we have but to open the ears and the eyes of our heart to be able to see and hear.

We would accept these words were it not for our desire for this world. Desire for this world closes the ear and self-interest closes the eye. Physical life is short. but *the essence of life* is long. What we need in this life is patience.

There was a small village in Turkey, and it was the local custom for the parents to marry off their children at a young age. So this man who was a poor farmer married his young son to one of the girls of the village, and there was a wedding feast. Everyone came, and on that night there was a group of men of knowledge who were passing through town, and they were invited and attended the wedding feast. As the festivities went on, they began to speak and soon gathered a small circle of listeners. This activity drew the attention of Ihsan, the young groom, and he went over to join them. He listened, and was astonished at what these men were saying. He had never heard anyone speak of this kind of knowledge.

After listening for a while, he said, "Where did you learn this? How did you come about this?"

And they said, "When we were very young, our parents wanted us to gain knowledge, so they sent us to Istanbul. We spent many years there, studying and applying the knowledge that we learned. Now we're on our way back to our villages, and we just happened to be passing through and that's why we're here now."

Ihsan was taken aback. At that moment, on his wedding night, he decided that the next day he was going to leave for Istanbul, and go there to seek and gain knowledge. At that moment he believed he could accomplish this quickly and easily and in no time he would return to his village. So Ihsan spent the wedding night with his bride. In the morning he informed her that he was leaving her in charge of the farm, she knew how to tend the fields and how to milk the cows, and as for himself he was going to Istanbul to gain knowledge. He assured her and told her not to worry, it wouldn't take too long. He'd be back shortly.

So Ihsan left. Well, it took three months to get to Istanbul, because traveling was difficult in those days. He was poor, and he had to walk. Finally he got there, and as the schools were free, he entered one and began his quest to attain knowledge.

Time went by, and before he knew it, years had passed, and he was still learning. He stayed on. Soon he forgot about his village, and he even forgot about his bride. He just stayed on, and studied hard. Ihsan badly wanted to have knowledge.

Thirty years passed. He became a middle-aged man. The time came when he felt that he had obtained enough knowledge, and he could now go back to his village. During all these years he had had no communication with the village nor with his family or friends. There was just no means at that time, it was too difficult.

One morning he decided to prepare for the long journey back to his village. He packed some food and, since he knew he would be traveling alone, he bought himself a gun for protection from the wild animals on the road. And he went off.

On the fifteenth day of his trip back to his own village, just around sunset he approached a farm, and there he saw an old farmer who was tilling the earth. Ihsan had graduated school and of course was wearing long robes, with his hat wrapped in the manner that symbolized a man of knowledge and which could be recognized by outsiders.

The old farmer Yunus immediately recognized this and with great deference said to him, "Oh, please, you're a man of knowledge, you're traveling on the road, be my guest. Stay at my house for a few days, rest, we'll feed you and take care of you."

Ihsan said, "Fine."

Old Yunus finished tilling the earth, he carried Ihsan's books and the rest of his traveling gear back into his house. The farmer's wife prepared him a wonderful meal. That night after dinner, as they were having coffee, old farmer Yunus said, "You know, I'm so happy you came. I've been waiting for a man of knowledge to come by here, because I have this burning question inside of me."

Ihsan became all puffed up and said, "Well, ask me. I've just spent thirty years obtaining all this knowledge. You know, that's why I'm here. No doubt Allah has sent me here for this purpose, to answer your burning question."

The old farmer said to him, "The question I have is: What is the beginning of knowledge?"

The other quickly replied, "Well, that's easy. The beginning of knowledge is *Bismillah*." *Bismillah* means in the Name of Allah, meaning that one should begin all things in the Name of Allah.

"No, no," old Yunus said, "that's just the beginning of the phrase of unity. That's not the beginning of knowledge."

65

"Oh, now I understand what you meant." He paused, then added, "The beginning of knowledge is preparing to do things in the right way."

"No, no," the old man exclaimed, "that just has to do with doing things in the right way. What I'm interested in knowing is what is the beginning of knowledge."

Ihsan began getting a little tense, and he said, "I don't know if I can answer your question."

And it disturbed him greatly, because he had just gone through this enormous training for thirty years. He had grown old in the city. He had given up his wife, his family, his village, and everything.

Finally, the old man looked at him and said, "I can tell you the answer to this question."

"All right, tell me," Ihsan said.

"Well, I just can't tell you that easily. If you work here for a year without pay in my fields, at the end of that time, I will tell you the meaning of the beginning of knowledge."

Now Ihsan was hooked. The fish doesn't go after the hook, the fish goes after the bait, never seeing that the hook is there. The old man baited him with the question about the beginning of knowledge, and he couldn't leave.

At that point he had no choice. And so he started working for old farmer Yunus. Ihsan worked hard, long days in the fields. Also, the meals were not the same as when he was a guest that first night. Usually there were a few olives, some soup, rice, and some tea. He continued to work hard, because the old man didn't let up on him. He worked for an entire year, day in and day out.

At the end of the year, Ihsan came to the old man and he declared, "The year is up. Please, now fulfill your obligation to me, since I've fulfilled mine to you. Tell me... tell me what is the beginning of knowledge?"

"I'll tell you in the morning just before you leave," old Yunus said casually.

"You mean it's going to be that quick, that short, like that? You're going to be able to tell the answer just as I'm leaving?!"

Old Yunus said, "Yes, just like that."

Ihsan had a sleepless night, as one can well imagine. He got up in the morning, and went to the kitchen where a nice breakfast had been prepared for him.

Old Yunus smiled at his wife, "Prepare some good food for the traveler to take on the road with him."

She prepared a bag. Ihsan sat down and just waited. After a while, he asked Old Yunus, "Now tell me, what is the beginning of knowledge?"

Old Yunus spoke slowly, "The beginning of knowledge is patience."

Ihsan was startled. "What! You tricked me! You made me work in your fields for a year, for nothing. And now you tell me something I myself have preached for years. I've taught this myself in schools and mosques! Taught that patience is important, that patience is knowledge. And now, after all this time, you're telling me—" he stopped abruptly.

Old Yunus, with a dismissing wave of the hand, said, "Just remember that the beginning of knowledge is patience." And without further ado he sent him off.

After that Ihsan had to travel for a long time, months more, before he finally reached the village of his long-ago youth. He could barely recognize it, so much time had passed. But somehow he managed to find his house. Ihsan hesitated before entering his house, thinking: Well, I don't even know who lives there now. I'd better look through the window. So he went and looked in the window, and there he saw his wife in the arms of this handsome young man. They were embracing and kissing. Ihsan got extremely angry and pulled out his pistol. Just as he was about to shoot and perhaps kill them, he remembered that the beginning of knowledge is patience. So he put his pistol away and went to the local coffeehouse. He sat there sipping good hot coffee and started making inquiries about some of his old friends. The villagers responded by saying that some had passed away some time ago, you know, so-and-so had moved away, and oh yes, this one is in the crazy house, and on and on the villagers went.

Finally, he got around to asking about himself, "What about that crazy young fellow, Ihsan, who went to get knowledge in Istanbul?"

And they said, "We haven't heard from him in thirty years. Nobody knows where he is. When he left, his wife had a very hard time. But she was such a good and faithful woman that she brought up their son, who was conceived on their wedding night, in such a way that he gained tremendous knowledge, and he's now the *imam*, the priest, of our mosque. He should be coming in here soon."

They went on talking, and presently this handsome young man who was *imam* of the mosque walked into the coffeehouse. And at that moment, Ihsan realized that the *imam* was his son. He realized that it was his son who was embracing his mother, the wife he had left thirty years ago. He left the coffeehouse and went out onto the road where, in a perplexed state, he wandered, grateful for having listened to old man Yunus, thankful for having been taught that the true beginning of knowledge is patience.

After some further reflection he went back to the coffeehouse and talked to his son and told everyone his story, and in closing he said, "I knew that the beginning of knowledge was patience. But I didn't understand it in the way that this old man Yunus taught it to me. Because of the way I understood it now, it saved the lives of my wife and my son."

So the beginning of knowledge is patience. A quality that would be good for everyone to acquire. Patience is a staff you can lean on. Allah is pleased with those who are patient.

Within all of us we have the staff of Moses. We also have the staff that turned into the snake. Within us we have Moses as well as

68

Pharaoh. Let Moses be the one who is victorious within us.

Within Sufism there's something called *adab*, proper spiritual conduct. *Adab* is spiritual courtesy. It's practiced in the circle of the dervishes. It's practiced among the people. Sufism is *adab*. There is an *adab* that is shown the stranger and the visitor, there is an *adab* that is due to the Sufi brotherhood, *fuqara*. Fuqara (coming from the word *fakir*) means he who is poor next to his Lord.

There's *adab* for the noble. There is an *adab* for the sheikh, for the spiritual guide. But *adab*, spiritual courtesy, is never complete until you complete the *adab* toward yourself. For true *adab* is spiritual consciousness. The world does not require *adab*, only good manners.

Mevlana Jelaluddin Rumi said, "If you are looking for a friend who is faultless, you will be friendless."

There was a young man who had a group of friends who were not very good. They took him in a direction which was not pleasing to his father. Finally one day his father said to him, "Look, my son, get rid of your friends. I'm going to teach you the meaning of friendship." The son obeyed and abandoned his friends. His father took him to the back of the house, and there he killed a sheep. He slit the throat of the sheep, took his bloody carcass, and he put it into a huge sack. One could see bloodstains soaking through the canvas cloth.

"Now, my son," he said, "you know Ahmet who lives down the road. We're the best of friends, as you know. Go and bring this sack to him, and tell him that your father accidentally killed someone. And ask him to help dispose of the body."

The young man took the sack, and carried it down the road to Ahmet's house. He knocked, and Ahmet opened the door.

"I'm the son of Habib," the young man announced. "There's been a terrible accident. My father has killed someone. The body is in this sack. My father asks that you help him dispose of this body, please!"

"Wait a minute," Ahmet said, and went back into his house. Soon he returned with a sack filled with gold coins. Handing them over, he said, "Here, take this to your father. With this money he will surely be able to get someone to dispose of this body." The son went back to his father and told him the story.

His father said, "My son, this is half a friend." Then he continued, "Now take this sack and tell the same story to Hussein who lives on the other side of town. You remember him, we were once very good friends. But lately we've disagreed on a lot of things, and actually in the last several months we haven't even spoken to each other. But take it to him."

He took the sack, walked across town, and knocked at Hussein's door. When the door opened, the young man said, "I'm the son of Habib. There's been a terrible accident. My father killed someone. The body is in this sack. He asked if you could please help him dispose of the body."

Hussein looked at the boy, grabbed the sack, and pushing him away, said, "Tell your father I'm not interested in him. And you, get out of here. Don't ever tell anyone you've seen me!" He slammed the door shut, but he kept the bloody sack.

The young man went home. He told his father the story of what had happened with Hussein. His father smiled and said, "That, my son, is a friend."

At the time of the Ottoman Empire in Turkey, one of the viziers told the sultan about a great sheikh who lived in Anatolia. He warned the sultan to be careful of this sheikh, because he had hundreds of thousands of followers. And if this sheikh decided to turn against the sultan, the whole country could be in turmoil and he could even lose his throne.

The sultan got quite concerned. He sent for the sheikh to come to Istanbul. When they met, the sultan said, "What is this I hear, you have hundreds of thousands of dervish followers?"

"No, that is not so," the sheikh answered.

"Well, how many do you have?" the sultan insisted.

"I only have one and a half."

"If you only have one and a half, why is everyone telling me that you have the power to overthrow this entire country? We shall see. There's a huge field at the edge of town, and tomorrow everyone is going to meet at that field."

The sultan sent out messengers to announce that anyone who was a follower of this great sheikh should come to this field the next day, because the sheikh would be there.

Above the field there was a hill where the sultan set up a huge tent. Inside the tent he put several sheep, but no one could see this.

The next day hundreds of thousands of people came to the field to see the great sheikh. In front of the tent the sultan stood next to the sheikh and said, "You said you didn't have many followers. Look at all these people who believe they're your followers."

"They are not," the sheikh said. "I only have one and a half dervishes. You'll see."

"The sheikh has committed an indiscretion," the sultan said. "And unless ten of his dervishes give up their life for him, his life will be taken."

There was a great rumbling in the crowd. "He is my sheikh and teacher. Whatever I know came from him," one man came forward and said. "I will go and give my life for him."

The sultan's men marched him up the hill, took him into the tent, and slit the throat of a sheep. Everybody saw the blood flowing out from the side of the tent, and this made them very nervous.

The sultan declared, "Is there anyone else willing to give his life for his sheikh?"

Silence.

Then one woman stood up and said she would. They marched her up and into the tent, and again they slit the throat of another sheep. Seeing more blood, the crowd began to disperse. Soon there was no one left in the field.

71

The sheikh turned to the sultan and said, "You see, I told you, I only had one and a half dervishes."

The sultan said, "Oh, the man is your dervish, and the woman is half a dervish?"

"No, no," the sheikh said. "The woman is my dervish, and the man is half a dervish."

Seeing the surprised expression on the sultan's face, the sheikh explained: "The man did not actually know that he was going to be killed when he entered the tent. But the woman knew, and she still came forward. She is my real dervish."

That is loyalty. Loyalty and friendship go together. We have to understand how to be friends. We wish to know Allah, but we don't know ourselves. We must begin to see in a way that we can learn about ourselves. Learn about this blessing that Allah has given us. Because we are, each of us, a blessing. Allah has placed a part of His Beauty in each one of us. And what He has not given to one person, He's given to another.

Often, we can see someone and be attracted to him almost immediately without knowing anything about him. Sometimes even without getting a real picture of what he looks like. It's the part of the beauty of Allah that is in us that is responding to the beauty of Allah that is within him.

This body is a miracle. We have to learn to read the book of ourselves. What does this book tell us? We have two eyes an inch apart that can see stars in the sky that are hundreds of thousands of miles away. We have eyebrows that are placed above our eyes so that when we work hard physically and sweat, the sweat doesn't go into our eyes. We have a nose that's placed above our mouth so that we can smell whether the food is good for us to eat. We have two kinds of teeth that Allah has given us, the front ones that bite and the side ones that chew.

Can we not see the miracle that we are? See that Allah has not given these gifts to any other creature in the world?

Allah has many Names, but there are ninety-nine Names, or Attributes, that are commonly known. On the palms of every person's hand are the numbers 81 and 18 in Arabic ciphers, and they add up to 99. Allah has placed a note for us—if you like, a reminder—that his Names are engraved, etched, in the palms of our hands. So that when we greet someone, or begin work, or embrace someone, or even if we think of hitting someone, if in that moment we know, if we can be aware that the Names of Allah are engraved on our hands, perhaps we would act differently.

Allah has left traces of His Essence for us to read on the planet, on our bodies, within us. If you see the prints of a camel in the sand of the desert, you don't have to see the camel to believe that the camel exists.

There once was what appeared to be a strange man, curious in the sense that in the living room of the house he lived in was a rope hanging from one of the rafters with a noose at the end of it. Every once in a while his son, as he grew up, would question his father about why this noose was hanging from the ceiling. The father said, "In time you will understand why the noose is there."

The son grew up, the years passed, and during this time the father had amassed a fortune. He had never explained the reason for the noose. Then suddenly one day he died. And the father had not left any clue for the son, hinting as to why the noose was there. But he had inherited the vast fortune. With that fortune, he also inherited numerous friends that he didn't have before. These friends really liked him and took him to many places of entertainment. Everywhere they went he always paid for everything. Obviously they liked him primarily for his money.

The young man was confused. In no time all of his money was gone. And so were his friends. They just disappeared. And he became lonely. One day sitting in the living room he realized that the noose was really meant for him. He became so despondent that he proceeded to hang himself. He tightened the noose around his neck, and jumped off a chair. As he crashed to the floor, the entire ceiling fell on his head, and with it baskets and baskets of money fell from the ceiling. And with it also a note from his father.

The note read:

My dear son, I knew that when, upon my death, you gained all this money, you would also gain friends who were not really your friends. I also knew that this day would come and that you would come to this rope. Now, I want you to understand that real friendship is not based on what you've based it on. Now take this money and use it wisely. Go into the world and help others. Don't be lured by those who just want to take advantage of you.

Soon it became known that he had amassed another fortune. Somehow, miraculously, all these friends reappeared. And they began to treat him as before. Once again they took advantage of his money. Sometimes they didn't even allow him to join them during their nights about town. One night they went so far as to say, "We're going out to the coffeehouse. You take this meat we've bought with your money and cook us a huge kabob. When we come back, we'll have a feast."

He stayed in the kitchen. As he was preparing the vegetables, the cat came in, snatched the meat, and ate it. It was all gone. His friends came back and hearing this news, got angry. "Where's the kabob? Where's the feast you promised—why aren't we sitting down to eat?"

He told them that he intended to please them all with a kabob but the cat had eaten the meat. They all got angry and began to beat him. Then he got smart. Finally. He said, "Wait a minute."

In the attic, he had discovered a sword. The sword had a very jagged edge. He showed the sword to all of his friends, because it was an antique.

They all said, "It's a beautiful sword, and it's worth a lot, but how did it get these jagged edges?"

And he said, "Oh, it's been in the attic for many years, and the

74

mice just chewed away at it."

"That's fantastic, imagine mice chewing through steel."

In turn, he said, "Look, my friends, you don't seem to doubt that mice can chew through steel and yet you don't believe that the cat ate the meat."

There was silence, they all looked at each other, and then he threw them out, and began his life anew.

Friendship can be wonderful. We have to understand the impulses that give it birth and what is involved.

If we look for a rose without thorns, we'll have a problem. Allah put thorns on the stem to protect the rose.

With beauty there is also pain. But this life just cannot be an endless fulfillment of joy. If we have faith in Allah, then whatever afflictions come to us, we will not be affected by them, we will not nourish them with our attention. If we are feeling lonely, and we feed that loneliness with our attention, it will grow. Faith in Allah is an inoculation against loneliness.

A Sufi was walking by a madhouse. He looked up, and there was a doctor leaning out of the window. He asked the doctor, "Have you discovered the cure for all that afflicts these men?" The doctor said he hadn't.

One of the crazy inmates was at the next window peering out, and he said, "Do you mind if I answer that question?" The doctor and the Sufi exchanged looks and said, "No! Not at all."

And the inmate said: "In the pharmacy of Allah, prescribed by Muhammad, you take the root of repentance and the leaf of consciousness. Grind them in the pestle of your heart, add some tears, sift it through your intelligence, cook it with the fire of your heart, taste it with a measuring spoon, then eat it with satisfaction."

He had given them a dervish recipe.

In the pharmacy of Allah. In the world we live in, prescribed by Muhammad, the doctor, one who was a messenger and sent to show good ways, to educate, to bring a message of Allah. Take the root of repentance. When you take the root of something, it's hard and knobby and difficult to pull out of the earth. But once you've uprooted it, it doesn't grow back. The leaf of consciousness weighs very little. This leaf, you can take only a little bit of it. You grind it in the pestle of your heart. You add some tears, your own tears. This life is feeling the presence of Allah in your repentance.

Then you sift it through your intelligence. Because your intelligence will tell you if it is right. Then cook it in the fire of your heart, in the warmth of your heart. We have said that Allah, who cannot fit into the entire universe, can fit into the heart of a believer. So you cook this potion in the fire of your heart. You taste it with a measuring spoon. Just a little, carefully. And then eat it with satisfaction. You take it into the world, and live according to the recipe.

Last year while traveling in Madinah, we met a man selling odds and ends on the street. We sat down to talk with him. It turned out he was a dervish. He told us of a man from Kayseri. He shined shoes for a living. He was a great dervish. He was simply hidden.

Once he had come to visit Madinah, and he met a man who told him, "Oh, it would be so wonderful if you could stay here. This is the place of the tomb of the Prophet, and you know, it's just the most wonderful place. There are great blessings. Why don't you come live here?"

His answer at the time was, "Then who will take care of the people in Kayseri?"

There are hidden beings who take care of people. There are *alim*, men of knowledge. This is the dervish who said he was convinced that Allah loved him because, he reasoned, how could you not love that which you have created?

Allah loves each one of us. Allah has created us. We're not here by accident. This world is a perfect design. If we can see it. If we can see ourselves and our surroundings. A vast sky held up by no pillars. A carpet of earth that gives us all the food and fruit and nourishment we need to live. Animals of every species. Some that

76

we can ride, some that we can eat, some that can help us in our work. They have specific duties. You can't tie a lion to a cart.

They've all been placed here as a means for us to see our inner natures. Just because we are dressed like human beings does not exempt us from having animal tendencies. The mouse in us that steals a little bit from here and there. The vain peacock that grooms himself all the time. The sly fox. The stubborn donkey that closes his ear to the Name of Allah. The scorpion that stings. These are all in us.

Human beings have the opportunity and the possibility not only to brush all that away but to become real human beings both internally and externally. If we reflect, and many of us do, why are we here? What is our purpose in this life? We didn't ask to come here. We find ourselves here. These are questions that we could ask throughout our lives, and many people have asked them with great confusion.

Allah said, "I was a hidden treasure, and I wished to be known. So I created man in order to be known." In that statement, Allah says that He has given us the possibility, the potential, the guidance and support that we need to know Him. Man can know Allah.

It is our purpose in this life to have faith, to worship, and to love Him. And also to fear Him. Although He is all-merciful and most forgiving, He can be feared.

The mouse fears the cat, not the lion. The man of the world fears the policeman, not Allah. Allah is too great.

We have come to a place of understanding in order to know our love and our fears. We are under the protection of Allah. This world, this life is a place we are just passing through.

We have to learn to serve one another. Service is the heart of Sufism. You must want more for your brother than you want for yourself, and, more important, before you want it for yourself.

Abu Yazid al-Bistami was a great Sufi sheikh. He was a *pir*, and known as the *Kutub al-Arifin*, the central pillar of knowledge, the man of the highest knowledge. One day in the courtyard of the mosque, he was making his ablutions in preparation for prayer. Across the courtyard, he saw a very old man. Today we have faucets that can be turned on, and the water simply flows, but in the old days they used heavy clay pitchers for water, and if you were strong enough, you picked one up and washed yourself. Often the person next to you would help you pour the water, and in turn you did the same for him.

What Abu Yazid al-Bistami saw was that no one was helping the old man. He walked over to the old man and said, "Old man, what could you have done in your long life that you do not have one friend, no one has come to help you?"

The old man looked at him and said, "The ones who serve are served. And if I had not served Allah and His creation, how would the *Kutub al-Arifin*, the man of the highest knowledge, come now to serve me?"

THE GLASS OF WATER

There's a story about a sheikh who was walking with one of his *murid*s, near a huge field. In the field there was a man who was digging holes. This man had dug two hundred holes two feet deep. Observing this, the *murid* asked, "O my sheikh, what is he doing?"

"I don't know. Let us ask him," the sheikh answered. They called him over, and asked what was the purpose of digging so many holes just two feet deep.

"I'm looking for water," the man said.

The sheikh told him, "It's unlikely that you will find water by digging two hundred holes that are only two feet deep. You have a better chance of finding water if you dig one hole two hundred feet deep."

When you choose a path, if your heart responds to that path, whatever it might be, and you have a true teacher, dig in that hole. By jumping from one path to another, you may touch the periphery of a lot of things, but you'll just obtain surface knowledge. Accepting a path is a commitment. It is like digging a two-hundred-foot-deep hole. When you dig one hole, when you accept one teaching, whatever it might be, you also have to understand that in digging that hole there are many obstacles. You'll find stones, stumps, roots, mud, and clay. At times it will be easy and at times it will be difficult. If you keep digging, and the path is true, with the help of Allah you will find water. You will come to knowledge and the Truth.

This is important to realize, because for many years there have been many offerings. But once you've decided on a Path, dig it until you're certain that it's not for you or that you've found the Truth. The search for Truth is often more important than the Truth itself.

The Truth has been given to us, and shared by many who have come before us. By Abraham, Jesus, Moses, Muhammad, may the peace and blessings of Allah be upon them. They have all brought the Truth. If the Truth were something you could just see or hear, it would be simple. But in the act of searching and discovering, each of us individually could find the Truth. The act of discovery will give us the strength and the understanding of knowing what to do with the Truth once we've found it.

There is a story that, if heard correctly, is the essence of Sufism.

One of the *khalifa*s of Hazrati Nureddin al-Jerrahi, the *pir* of the Halveti-Jerrahi order of dervishes, was a man named Moravi Yahya. He had spent a lot of time in Morea, where he opened over forty *tekke*s, dervish lodges.

At the age of 110, he came back to Istanbul and began to teach in one of the dervish *tekke*s.

Some of his dervishes knew of a man named Haydar who wanted to become a dervish. These dervishes kept asking the sheikh if Haydar could come to the *tekke*. Finally, the sheikh said, "Let him come for a while and stay in the outer room, and if he likes it, let him just continue to come."

After several months, Haydar was once again anxious and asked to become a dervish of the sheikh. Finally Sheikh Moravi Yahya said, "Bring him next Thursday night."

The process of taking hand with a sheikh is the initiation into Sufism. You sit knee to knee with the sheikh, take his hand, and a transmission occurs. You become linked, not only to that sheikh, but to the entire chain of sheikhs that go all the way back to the Prophet Muhammad.

When you take hand with a sheikh, you take the hand of the hand of the hand of the hand that held the hand of the Prophet

Muhammad. Haydar wanted to take hand with the sheikh. On the next Thursday, his friends brought him, and the sheikh said to one of his *murids*, "Have him bring me a glass of water."

His dervish friends took him aside, and they showed him exactly how to hold the glass, how to approach the sheikh, and how to serve him correctly. He practiced in the back near the tea service room until he felt he was ready.

In order to reach the sheikh at the head of the crowded room, Haydar had to sidestep hundreds of people.

He's walking carefully, holding the glass full of water in the palm of his hand. Slowly he makes his way through the crowd. Finally, he reaches the sheikh. He bows and stretches out his hand to give the sheikh the water. Suddenly the sheikh, while talking, waves his hand and knocks over the glass. The water flies through the air. In that very moment, Haydar is transported to the edge of a cliff near a city that he's never seen.

He made his way down the valley, toward the city. When he reached the city, he realized he was hungry. He found a restaurant, went in and ordered a meal. When he was finished, he reached into his pockets for money. At this time, the restaurant owner approached him and asked, "What are you doing? What are you looking for?"

"I'm looking for money to pay for the meal," Haydar said.

"Oh, there's no payment here. In this village there's no payment. You just have to say *Bismillah ir-Rahman ir-Rahim*."

"*Bismillah ir-Rahman ir-Rahim*," Haydar said, and he felt terrific. Then he added, "This is a wonderful place. Right? I mean you don't have to pay for a meal, you say *Bismillah ir-Rahman ir-Rahim*, that's easy."

With those words on his lips, he decided to have another cup of coffee, and then even another. When he was about to leave, the waiter said, "Wait a minute! With this cup of coffee, you have to recite a *Fatiha*."

The *Fatiha* is the opening chapter of the Quran. It's very short.

Not too difficult. So Haydar said the *Fatiha*, went on his way, thinking and feeling that this was very good . . . very good indeed.

While walking he observed that his clothes had become ragged. He came upon a clothing store, walked in, and tried on a new set of clothes. The shopkeeper was courteous and attentive. When he was ready to pay, the shopkeeper said, "No, no! We don't accept money anywhere in this village. These clothes are yours. You just have to recite the *sura Ya Sin*."

Sura Ya Sin is a very long chapter. Haydar felt the price to be a little steeper than what he paid for the cup of coffee. But still it was reasonable. He recited the *sura Ya Sin*. Which is the *sura*, or chapter, usually recited when someone dies.

The shopkeeper observed him and said, "You're obviously new to this village."

And Haydar answered, "Yes, I am. I just arrived today. I don't really know the ways of your village."

"You probably don't even have a place to stay."

"No, I don't."

The shopkeeper smiled, "I have a little room on top of the store, and you're welcome to use it."

Haydar thanked him.

That night, before retiring, the shopkeeper told Haydar the following: "Now look, the only thing you have to do is lock your door before you go to sleep. Then take this candle, light it, and place it in the window. The women of the village come at night, and the candles light their way for them to take anything they need."

Haydar did as he was told. And there he stood looking out of the window watching the procession of women. Out of the crowd, he spotted one woman. She just caught his eye. He fell in love with her immediately.

Although the bed was nice and soft, he couldn't sleep. The next morning, the shopkeeper came to see him and asked, "Well, how did it go?"

Haydar smiled, "Everything was fine. Sort of . . . well, I saw this woman, well, I just fell in love with her. How can I meet her?"

"That's easy. Tonight take these two candles. Place one in the window. When you see the women coming, take the other candle, go outside, and hand it to her. If she accepts that light from you, then other arrangements will be made."

That night, he placed one candle in the window and waited patiently for the women of the village to arrive. When they did, he spotted his beloved and ran downstairs with the second candle. With a trembling hand and an open heart he handed it to her. She accepted it.

He went back to his room feeling ecstatic. But now he didn't know what to do next. The following morning, the shopkeeper came to see him and asked, "How was it last night?"

"I didn't sleep very well again, but she took the candle. Now what do I do?"

"Have patience."

So he waited patiently. Later that day there was a knock at the door. He heard voices asking, "Are you Haydar?"

"Yes."

"The chief justice of the village would like to see you."

He was frightened, but he gathered his courage and went to the courthouse.

The chief justice sat before him and said, "I understand that you want to marry my daughter."

Haydar said, "Yes. Well, I would love to marry her."

The chief justice said, "Fine, she has accepted you. But before you marry her, there are three conditions you have to adhere to in order to live in this village.

"The three conditions are: One, you cannot steal. You cannot take anything from anyone that does not belong to you. Two, you cannot lie. And three, you cannot lust after another woman."

Haydar thought it over. It sounded like a reasonable set of demands. He was going to get this beautiful woman as his wife, and he willingly agreed to all the conditions.

There was a big and festive wedding. He was provided with work. Everything went along fine for a long time. Then one day Haydar and his wife went on a picnic in a large field by the woods. He was coming back from a walk, eating an apple he had found.

"Where did you get that apple?" his wife asked abruptly.

"From over there on the ground," he said.

"You stole that apple," she said. "That apple belongs to the person on whose land it is."

"Well," he said, "it wasn't on the tree. I didn't pluck it from the tree. It was just on the ground."

"Nevertheless," she said, "you took something that didn't belong to you. I have to leave you."

He said, "Look, I'll do anything. I just made a mistake. I wasn't aware that it was that serious. I just—"

She packed her bags and left. He was heartbroken. He didn't know what to do.

He was brought before the chief justice, who told him, "Look, this is a grave mistake. Nobody here steals anything. You cannot take what does not belong to you."

"I really made a mistake, please, forgive me. I don't want to lose my wife."

The chief justice said, "Because you are new here, we will forgive you this one time. But it can never happen again."

He was elated for having been forgiven, and in addition there was no punishment. He went home, and his wife moved back into the house. Everything was fine. Several years went by, and they lived happily. Then one morning, there was a knock on the door. It was early, and he was still in bed. His wife answered the door. It was a friend who wanted to see him, and she came back into the bedroom and said, "Your friend is here, and he'd like to see you."

He rolled over and said, "Tell him I'm not here."

"You lied," she said, and without another word, she packed her bags and left again. Again he was distraught. Again he came before the chief justice, who told him, "You have now sinned twice. You've gone against the ways of our village twice. This is a place which cannot accept this kind of behavior."

"But I was tired," Haydar said. "I just rolled over in bed and told her to tell him I wasn't home. I simply wanted another hour's sleep."

"Yes, but you have to understand that it was a lie," the chief justice said. "And this time, we cannot forgive you so easily."

Haydar was punished, but allowed to remain in the village. He was warned that he could not make any other mistakes.

Time went by and they lived happily. His wife was back with him. And slowly they grew old together. Many years had elapsed. His wife had lost much of her youthful beauty, and this made him unhappy. As of late he had made it a habit to walk by the river. Occasionally he would look through the trees and peer out at the young girls who were bathing in the river. One day someone saw him. They told his wife and once again she left him. And once again he was brought before the chief justice.

This time the chief justice said, "Now you have lusted. You have failed to recognize the beauty of your wife. You went to find feminine beauty in another. You have broken all three guiding principles of how we live in this village. You must be banished. There is no more forgiveness."

He was taken by two strong men and dragged to the top of the mountain . . . to the precipice where many years earlier he had first appeared. They each took him by one arm and leg and began to swing him back and forth. With one sweeping movement they threw him out of the village. Just as they let go and he felt himself floating in the air, at that moment he once again found himself standing before the sheikh, and he could see the water pouring out of the glass.

85

The sheikh looked at him and said, "How good a dervish can you be when you cannot even serve your sheikh a glass of water?"

It is a story to think about.

A *hadith* tells of a man coming to the Prophet and asking, "O, my Prophet, please give me the one thing that will help me in this life."

The Prophet reached out and grabbed his tongue. He said, "Hold your tongue. It will give you safety and comfort in this life."

That is why Allah has placed our words in a mouth that imprisons them by rows of teeth, hard teeth that clamp shut. And lips that seal the mouth. Words don't have to flow out of your mouth as quickly as they sometimes do.

IF ALL THE OCEANS WERE INK

It is a difficult task to go through one complete day saying only what you mean. You can experience this on your own. If you choose to do it, I suggest you do it on a day when the world is not going to capture you, and you're not going to see many people. It will give an indication of how asleep and how insensitive we are. How frequently we speak about useless things. How we waste a great deal of time and a great deal of this precious life. I'm not saying that we should not be entertained and enjoy life. But if we examine how many conversations we have in a day that are absolutely useless and meaningless, it will give us a clearer picture of ourselves. This is extremely important within every path, not only in Sufism. We have to get to know ourselves.

In the entranceway to the Pythagorean school, there was a phrase that is very well known. It said, "Know thyself." But the second part of that phrase is not as well known. What was written at the entranceway was, "Know thyself always and everywhere."

How we use words affects not only us. It affects other people. We can transfer our anger to another person and can receive someone else's anger. We have to be selective and understand what we give to someone, how much and in what way.

There was a very devout woman. She was a Sufi, and whenever she did anything, she said *Bismillah*, in the Name of Allah. When she sat down, she said *Bismillah*, when she got up she said *Bismillah*. When she put something in the cupboard, she said *Bismillah*, when she took something off a shelf, she said *Bismillah*.

Her husband, who wasn't as enthusiastic, decided one day that he was going to teach her something about saying *Bismillah* all the time.

"Wife," he said, "here's a sack of gold. I want you to hold it for me." She took it and said *Bismillah*.

"Lock it away in the cupboard," he said. "When I ask for it, bring it to me."

She unlocked the cupboard, opened the door, and with every action she said *Bismillah*.

That night, when she was asleep, he opened the cupboard, took the sack of gold, and threw it down the well. The next day he said, "Wife, I now need that sack of gold I gave you to hold for me yesterday."

She went to the cupboard, *Bismillah*, she opened it, *Bismillah*, she reached in and brought out the sack of gold. It was soaking wet. She gave it to him and said *Bismillah*. He took it and said *Bismillah*.

Insha'Allah means God willing. We say this because we know that when we close our eyes at night it is possible that we may not wake up in the morning. Or if we wake up one morning, we may not be alive to go to sleep that night. So we say *Insha'Allah*, the Will of Allah.

The Prophet Muhammad was frequently, as were all the prophets, mistreated and tested by the people around him who didn't believe. We don't arrive at a religion easily. Other beings have suffered for us just to be let in the door. Whichever door it is. The Prophet Jesus endured great suffering. His companions were killed, thrown to the lions. He was crucified.

Long before, the Pharaoh destroyed the people of Moses. And this was a Pharaoh with an army and a kingdom. But what about the pharaohs we know in our own life, who have no army and no kingdom, but have that degree of pharaonic arrogance in life? What if they ever came to power?

Noah's jaw was broken. He was beaten. The Prophet Muhammad was poisoned. What we have inherited as a people, whatever path or religion we believe in and follow, has not come without great pain and struggle.

The Quraysh were the people of Makkah at the time of the Prophet Muhammad. They drove him away to Madinah, where he was accepted. Here was a man who couldn't read or write. Every year, in the month of Ramadan, he would go to the mountain, and there in one of the caves he would meditate for forty days. In his fortieth year, during one of these meditations, he heard a voice. And the voice said: *Read!*

And he said, I cannot read.

Again the voice said, Read!

He said, I cannot read.

Read!

What should I read?

Read in the Name of Allah, who has created you from a clod, a drop of water, and is the teacher of all men.

Not only could the Prophet not read, we also cannot read. That is, we cannot read on the level that is necessary for us. To read the traces that Allah has sent down to us, to read our own selves and become close to Him.

One day the Quraysh, who regarded the Jewish people as intelligent, went and asked them if they could think of three questions that they could ask the Prophet in order to disprove the knowledge he was reputed to possess.

They came with these three questions. First, they wanted to know the meaning of the story of the young men who left their village. Next, they wanted to know the name of the traveler who traveled far and wide to the East and West. Finally, they asked a question that they themselves wanted to know the answer to: What is the spirit?

The Prophet was asked the three questions. The answers were

not within his realm of knowledge, and not having received a divine answer, he said, "Come back tomorrow, and I'll tell you."

They came the next day, and again he had not received any message. He told them to come back the next day. And so this went on for fourteen days. The Prophet was becoming concerned that the answers were not coming to him. This was going to cast doubt among the people. Or was this really Allah's wish?

On the fifteenth day, the Angel Gabriel came and told him that Allah made him wait fifteen days for the answers because: "One is to say nothing of what one will do tomorrow without first saying *Insha'Allah.*" When they asked him these questions, the answers to which he did not know, and he said I'll tell you tomorrow, he should also have said *Insha'Allah.*

For the first answer he told the story of the sleepers of Ephesus. For believing in one God while others fell to idolatry, some young men were driven from their village and took refuge in a cave where they slept for three hundred years. The Prophet added to his answer a description of how the sleepers looked as they slept.

He told them that it was Dhul-Qarnayn who traveled far and wide to the East and the West. He told them the places where he actually traveled, which were not in the books.

As the answer to "What is the spirit?," he told them that Allah said the spirit is something that comes from Him. And that enough knowledge of it is given to human beings, and it was up to them to use it. If they didn't use that knowledge, any additional knowledge would be useless.

If we apply what we learn from the books to our lives, then Allah will teach us what cannot be found in books. Sufism is a continuous and daily application of a way of life.

It is said in the Quran: If all the trees on earth were pens, and if the ocean with seven oceans behind it were ink, the Words of Allah could not be written out to their end.

This is a story my sheikh told me about one of his teachers who was a sheikh in Yugoslavia. It was during Ramadan, the Islamic month of fasting. There once was a *hoja*, a teacher, who preached to the people every day in the mosque. One day he was talking about the importance of saying *Bismillah*, that this word held great power. With this word you could open enormous doors. With this word you could even walk across the lake in front of the mosque.

In the congregation was a man who lived on the other side of the lake. As he left that late afternoon, he began thinking: why should I walk around the lake? It takes me two hours to walk around the lake, I could say *Bismillah* and walk across the lake.

That day he said *Bismillah*, and he walked on the water across the lake. In the morning, on his way to the mosque, instead of taking the two-hour road, he said *Bismillah* and again walked across the lake. He went directly to the *hoja* and said, "*Hoja*, you are a wonderful teacher. I've gotten so much from you that I would like to invite you to *iftar* with my family tonight." As an invitation cannot be refused, the *hoja* said, "*Alhamdulillah, Insha'Allah*, we'll break the fast together."

At the day's end, they left the mosque and walked to the bank of the river. As he was about to cross he said, "Come on, *hoja*."

The *hoja* said, "Don't we have to go around the lake to get to your house on the other side?"

He said, "No, we'll say *Bismillah*, and walk across the lake."

He said *Bismillah*, and began walking across the lake. When he was about twenty feet out, he looked back, and seeing the *hoja* still on the shore, said, "Well, *hoja*, say *Bismillah* and come on."

The *hoja* said, "Wait a minute, I mean, I know I said that, but I don't think that I'm at the level where I can say *Bismillah* and walk on water." The man said, "All right, come, I'll carry you across."

He put the *hoja* on his shoulders, said *Bismillah*, and walked across.

Now, the *hoja* had book knowledge. The *hoja* had not experienced what he knew. The man was truly an *alim*, a man of knowledge and a true believer.

Once the sultan's daughter was sick. It was known that Pir Nureddin Jerrahi could heal people. The sultan sent for him. At court all the physicians were extremely upset that the sultan would send for a dervish sheikh. They said to him, "Look, there is nothing you will be able to do. We have given this child the best medicines available. We are the best physicians in the land. There is nothing that can be done to help her."

"I'll repeat the Name of Allah," Pir Nureddin said, "and breathe *Hu* over her."

The physicians said, "You must be joking. You are going to breathe on her and say the Name of Allah, and she will get better? Our medicine has failed, and you think you can succeed? That's impossible."

He looked at them and said, "Listen, you donkeys, you don't know anything." With these words, the physicians got so angry that their faces turned red. At any moment they were ready to attack him.

He said, "Why is it that if I call you a donkey, you become angry, but you won't accept the reality that the Name of Allah could make someone feel better?"

There is great power in the words we use. There was a man named Muadh, who was a companion of the Prophet Muhammad. Once they were riding on the same camel. Muadh was on the back.

The Prophet said, "Ya, Muadh, O Muadh."

And Muadh said, "Yes, O my Prophet."

They rode on and again the Prophet said, "Ya, Muadh."

"Yes, my Prophet." Again the Prophet didn't say anything. Indicating that what he was about to say was extremely important. Again the Prophet said, "Ya, Muadh."

And again Muadh leaned forward and said, "Yes, yes, my Prophet, at your service."

The Prophet said, "Know this. For anyone who says *La ilaha illa Allah*, there is no god but Allah, *Muhammadur Rasul Allah*, and Muhammad is His Messenger, there will be no punishment, and all will be forgiven."

Muadh quite excitedly said, "Is this something I can tell everyone?" The Prophet said, "No, don't tell it, because they will ease off on their work, and they will ease off on their prayer."

Muadh remained silent until, on his deathbed, he repeated what he had heard. Then it became a *hadith*, a tradition, something actually heard from the mouth of the Prophet Muhammad.

So there is great power in words. *La ilaha illa Allah*, there is no god but Allah, is called the *tawhid*. *Tawhid* means unity. It is the phrase of unity. It is the phrase that is recited in the *dhikr*. *Dhikr* means remembrance. The remembrance of Allah. There are only two reasons, two levels of remembering Allah. You remember Allah because you have forgotten Him, which is the condition that almost all of us are in. But there are those who always remember Allah. If they forget, even for a moment, it is like falling from grace.

The dervish repeats the *dhikr*, whether it be *la ilaha illa Allah*, or other Names of Allah, many times in his remembrance. If you say bread, bread, bread when you're hungry, this will not satisfy your hunger. But someone may hear your call and give you a piece of bread. If you say *la ilaha illa Allah*, it will be heard.

If someone fixed you a plate of poisoned food, and you believed that the poison would not harm you, would you die? You would die. But if you said *la ilaha illa Allah*, even if you didn't understand the true meaning of it, you would be saved.

Sufism was once a reality without a name. Today it is a name without a reality. This was said by a Sufi sheikh in the tenth century. Today, what the Sufis are doing is making Sufism a name with a reality.

There was a time when people lived according to the principles of Sufism. But this was forgotten. So the reality did not exist. They had a name for it, and it seemed the name was enough. We believe that it is enough to know *about* something. We believe that it is enough to know *about* a place, subject, or knowledge and wisdom that is the guidance for a way of life.

For instance. Let us take a place like Fairbanks, Alaska, and let us assume that we've all heard of it but that very few, if any, of us have ever been there. We may have heard of Fairbanks. We may even have seen photographs. Some of us may have seen a documentary that shows us the character of the land and the culture of the people. We have read many books and even met people from there—but all that this amounts to is information and *knowing about something.* Let us say that you decide to go to Fairbanks. You make all the travel arrangements, and this becomes the first step toward the reality that is Fairbanks. It is the first station of experience. But even at this moment all that you imagine about Fairbanks, combined with all that you have read and all the photos and the films you've seen, is only the first step of being on the way.

Next you are on the plane. You are actually on your way there . . . on your way to experience the reality, but not quite there, for the flight takes some six hours. During the flight, your thoughts about Fairbanks are beginning to change as you approach the experience of the reality. Soon the flight is about over and the captain is announcing the landing. Suddenly, after hours of flight, after many books and even more photos and films and a thousand preconceptions, you have finally arrived in Fairbanks. But now you are still only in the beginning of the reality. A reality that must compete with your imagination of what you believe Fairbanks was all these years.

Now you are living in Fairbanks and are getting to know the land and the people through firsthand experience. You don't have to read, you don't have to look at documentaries . . . you are now at the beginning of being part of Fairbanks. You are at the stage

94

of experiencing and discovering Fairbanks. If you manage to live there for many years, you might actually get to know it. The more years you spend, the more you'll know. And then one day, after living in Fairbanks for years, you might indeed decide to become a citizen of the city. And if you stay long enough, others might grow to believe you are the city. That is, all your action, your way of being totally represent the reality that is the Fairbanks experience.

What I have just described actually applies to all real experience and knowledge, whether it be spiritual or worldly. There are no short cuts, except by divine intervention. That is, if Allah wills, He can bestow certain knowledge upon you as a gift. The key is always to remember that it is a gift and Who was the giver.

What I have just described also describes the four stations of knowledge in *tariqa*, the Way of Sufism, and the four doors that every dervish must go through if he is to reach his personal spiritual perfection. They are as follows: *shari'a*, the indications of law as put forth in the Quran; *tariqa*, the spiritual path emblematic of being on the way; *haqiqa*, the Absolute Reality, living and experiencing the cloak of divine reality, living one's life according to that Reality; *ma'rifa*, becoming the Inner Truth of that Absolute Reality. In other words, in this last state, you and Fairbanks are interchangeable, but you are not Fairbanks.

I've gone through this at length because experience is a crucial aspect of Sufism—to be the Truth is much harder than to speak of the Truth, even eloquently. It is difficult to know something, because to know always requires actions. Anything else is merely information, and information when it comes to spiritual growth is useless. Action turns the information into knowledge, and that knowledge in time turns into wisdom. The experience of knowledge makes it wisdom. Knowledge can be forgotten, but wisdom is an experience from within that belongs to you. Just as once having gone and lived in Fairbanks will always be a part of you, even though at times you may forget . . . the experience will always be there and perhaps others will see it and be inspired to go to Fairbanks.

There exist many dervish orders. It is important to know that there is no such thing as one Sufi order. There are many Sufi orders, and all of them have evolved out of a particular individual.

The Qadiri order of dervishes, for instance, came from a man named Abdul Qadir Gilani. He did not start this order of dervishes. He did not initiate anyone. He did not make anyone a dervish. He was a man of knowledge who attended a Sufi school in his youth, went into the desert for twenty years and, when he came out, dressed not as a Sufi but as an *alim*, a man of knowledge. He taught in that manner. After he passed away, a dervish order grew out of the practices and indications he had given.

The same applies to Ahmed Rufai of the Rufai order of dervishes. He spent his entire life—except for the one trip of *hajj*, pilgrimage to Makkah—in the marshland of Iraq. He belonged to a hereditary chain of transmission. He was given the *hirka*, the cloak of the sheikh, and became the leader of a number of dervishes.

The Rufai dervishes are often called the howling dervishes, because of the way they do their *dhikr*. The sound of their *dhikr* is a heavy breath. The Halveti do *dhikr* in a similar manner, and they are also known at times as howling dervishes.

The Rufai were known for their ability to handle snakes, pierce themselves with swords and all sorts of sharp instruments. I've witnessed these feats. Once while in Istanbul, I went to visit a Rufai sheikh. He was eighty years old. He's moved on now. I was in the back of this *dergah*, dervish prayer lodge, when this old man was led in. He sat down beside me. I looked at him and thought, this is really an old man! They probably brought him here to be healed.

I soon discovered that he was the sheikh. After the evening prayer, everyone gathered and formed a *dhikr* circle. They placed me in front as I was a guest. This old sheikh was led to the center of the circle, and he started the *dhikr*. Reciting the attribute *Hayy*, the Everliving, he moved from person to person around the circle. Under his guidance and presence, the *dhikr* became very powerful. Some dervishes brought out a huge metal container, called a *mangal*, that holds hot coals taken from the fire and is used to keep the room warm. The coals were white hot. A poker was protruding from them. The old sheikh walked over to the hot coals. He took his false teeth out of his mouth and handed them to one of his dervishes. Then he took his jacket off and grabbed the hot poker— it was radiating white heat—and reciting the *destur*, the permission, he spat onto the poker. The poker made a loud hissing noise. It was *hot*. Then he proceeded to rub the hot poker between his hands. Then he licked it. This practice is called the Rufai Rose. He licked it and continued to lead the *dhikr*. He moved from one person to the next with the poker. As I watched him do the *dhikr*, the repetition of the Name of Allah, he seemed to have dropped forty years right before my eyes. He became a young man, energetically leading the *dhikr*, moving people all around the circle, so that the energy of the *dhikr* was balanced throughout. All the time, as he did the *dhikr*, he also kept on licking the white hot poker.

He had faith, and I witnessed it with my own eyes. This is a gift Allah has bestowed on the Rufai. How did this come to be? Sheikh Ahmed Rufai made his singular journey out of the Iraq marshland to go on *hajj*, to go to Makkah and Madinah to visit the tomb of the Prophet. It is incredible to be in a space with two million people all dressed in similar white cloths, praying in the same direction. It is an incredible experience.

At the time of Ahmed Rufai, there were perhaps 90,000 people who were making the pilgrimage, *hajj*. Ahmed Rufai left Makkah and went to Madinah where he stood before the tomb of the Prophet Muhammad, weeping and saying that he just wanted to serve—now we are talking about an older man, already in his sixties, a man who had spent his whole life in prayer, the leader of a Sufi order—asking how could he serve, asking and weeping. In

97

this state of tears and helplessness, Ahmed Rufai saw a hand come out of the tomb. Without hesitation, he ran over and kissed the hand. It was the hand of the Prophet Muhammad. The people around him also saw the hand. At this sight they went crazy. Just as they started to run over to it, the hand withdrew. At that moment, Ahmed Rufai said, "I cannot go on living. Take your sword, kill me," addressing one of his *murids*. "Stab me so I can die here." His dervishes stabbed him. They listened to him. Each one of them put a sword into him. Nothing harmed him. He didn't die, he didn't even bleed.

Ever since then, the sheikhs of the Rufai *tariqa* have had the ability to cut open their stomachs with knives, stick skewers through parts of their bodies, and lick white hot pokers. That was the gift given to Sheikh Ahmed Rufai, and his spiritual heirs inherited this gift.

There are other people in the world who can perform similar feats. Many of us have seen photographs and documentaries of such events. But the difference between a Rufai sheikh and these others is not only that he can perform these feats on himself, but he can also do the same to others without their feeling it. All this is a result of their immense power of faith, and Allah allows them to do it.

So we mentioned the Mevlevi, The Whirling Dervishes, and Jelaluddin Rumi, the Qadiri, Rufai, and we've talked a lot about the Halveti. These are just a few, and there are many more Sufi orders. Shadhilli, Naqshbandi, Bektashi.

There are a lot of interesting and funny stories about the Bektashis, because the Bektashis are reputed to be a little irreverent. Supposedly they drink wine and do things that are not exactly acceptable or considered the norm. Yet they are also viewed as holy beings. The Bektashi are an important dervish order.

There was once a Bektashi who stopped in a mosque. It was the first place he saw to shelter himself from the rain. As he stood there, it became time for the prayer. He joined in the prayer line. At the end of the prayer, he made a *dua*, a personal prayer. His *dua* consisted of the following: "O Allah, please, we're so hungry at home. Our family has no food. Won't You please bring some food for us to eat? Fill our table with fruits and vegetables and meats so that we can also enjoy the pleasures of being Your servants. And oh, by the way, Allah, when You send this servant to my house with all of this good food, would You ask him to bring a half a gallon of raki?" Raki is a licorice-tasting alcoholic drink.

In front of him was a man who upon hearing this prayer turned around and said, "You're asking Allah to bring you a half a gallon of raki? Why don't you ask Allah to give you more faith so that on the Day of Last Judgment you will be saved, so that you won't have the punishment of this world? Why don't you ask Him for more understanding of your religion?"

Without looking up, the Bektashi said, "Brother, I asked Allah for what's missing in my life. You ask Allah for what's missing in your life. If faith were missing in my life, I would ask Allah for faith. But raki is missing in my life."

That's the way the Bektashi are reputed to be.

Again, there was this Bektashi who stopped in a mosque. Probably he too was getting shelter from the rain. He was praying, and a man sitting next to him turned around and said, "You did something wrong in that prayer, and that prayer is not accepted."

The Bektashi looked at him and said, "That's all right. I didn't make that prayer to you."

The dervish wears special clothes. They all have a meaning. The shoes he wears are shoes with which you walk toward Allah. The long *tenure*, robe, he wears has twelve buttons that correspond to the twelve *imams* within the path. The other four buttons represent the four doors and the four sacred books that Allah has sent: the Torah, the Psalms, the Gospels, and Quran. The hats have particular designs in linear patterns sewn into them. Horizontally there are four lines that represent, again, the four books of Allah. They also represent the four doors, the four gates that are the four stations of knowledge. Some have five lines, and they represent the five pillars of Islam. They also represent *la ilaha illa Allah*. The special vest that is worn is called the *haydariyah*, which can be traced back to Imam Ali. The overall dress is white, so that any spot of dirt can be clearly seen. It is also a shroud. Because to be a real dervish is to die before dying. If you've read about Sufism, then you've heard the expression *to die before you die*.

What this really means is to die to all of the negation, to die to all that is harmful to us. It's not a physical death. But to die to worldly attachments and live within the light of Allah.

There is a special *adab*, proper spiritual behavior, between sheikhs of dervish orders. A man wanted to be a dervish. He went to see Sultan Veled, the son of Jelaluddin Rumi, in Konya, who was then the head of the Mevlevi order. Sultan Veled said, "*Alhamdulillah*, all praise is for Allah. Come, bring a sheep, and we will make a feast."

The man left, and the next Thursday he was supposed to bring a sheep. He was a thief. That was his job, so he stole a sheep. He threw the sheep over his shoulders and walked up to the door of the *tekke*. Sultan Veled stopped him and said, "Wait! That sheep cannot be cooked in our pots. You cannot be a dervish with our order."

The man was upset. He wandered the streets of Konya, until he met a friend, who, seeing his state, asked, "What's the matter?"

"Oh," he said, "I was going to be a dervish. Then I stole a sheep. How did he know I stole this sheep? I mean, he told me that a stolen sheep couldn't be cooked in their pots. But how did he know? I didn't tell him. He knew. Now I can't be a dervish."

His friend said, "Don't worry, go to the next town. No problem, there's a sheikh there, and he'll accept you as his dervish."

By now he was familiar with the procedure for becoming a dervish. Again he stole a sheep, flung it over his shoulders, and went to the next town. The sheikh there was named Hajji Bayram Veli.

100

He went to see the sheikh, who said, "Come. Come to my *tekke*. We cook everything in our *tekke*."

He also knew that this was a stolen sheep. But he accepted it. He invited him into the *tekke*. They had a big feast, and the thief was made a dervish.

Soon the man started getting a little smug and began thinking: I'll go back to Konya and see Sultan Veled, and show him that this great sheikh, Hajji Bayram Veli, accepted me when he wouldn't.

He went to the door of the Mevlevi *tekke*, and said, "Do you remember me?"

Sultan Veled said yes.

"You wouldn't make me a dervish," he said, "but Hajji Bayram Veli, the great sheikh, he made me his dervish."

And Sultan Veled said, "Hajji Bayram Veli is like a huge ocean, and one drop of dirt in the ocean can't be seen."

When he went back and saw Hajji Bayram Veli again, he said to him, "You accepted me. Why did you accept me when Sultan Veled didn't?"

"Ah, well," Hajji Bayram Veli said, "you see, Sultan Veled is so pure that even one speck of dirt can spoil his purity."

So we see that great honor exists among the dervish orders. They all work together. Although they have different sheikhs and different ways according to the cultural climate of their origin and geographic region, the common practice among all of them is the *dhikr*. The remembrance of Allah, and the obligatory prayers to Allah.

In the *dhikr* we repeat the words *la ilaha illa Allah* over and over again. We are saying there is no god but Allah. We are affirming that there is one God, and He has no equal and no partner. That a tree is not God. Allah is the only one to be worshiped.

As we repeat *la ilaha illa Allah* outwardly, in our minds we are thinking *Muhammadur Rasul Allah*.

The circle of *dhikr* belongs to the dervishes. For centuries it has been a form of prayer and remembrance of Allah. With the broom of *la ilaha illa Allah*, we sweep out all negative aspects from our hearts.

There is a *hadith kudsi*, a *hadith* with a message from Allah in it. This is on the authority of Abu Hurayrah, may Allah be pleased with him, from the Prophet Muhammad, may the blessings and peace of Allah be upon him, who said:

"Allah, glorified and exalted is He, has supernumerary angels who rove about seeking out gatherings in which Allah's Name is being invoked. The angels sit with them and fold their wings around each other, filling that which is between them and between the lowest heaven. When the people in the gathering depart, the angels ascend and rise up to heaven."

He said then, "Allah, mighty and sublime be He, asked them, though He is most knowing about them, 'From where have you come?' And they say, 'We have come from some servants of Yours on earth. They were glorifying You, exalting You, witnessing that there is no God but You, praising You and asking of You.' And Allah said, 'What do they ask of Me?' The angels say, 'They ask of You Your Paradise.' And Allah said, 'Have they seen My Paradise?' They say, 'No, O Lord.' And He says, 'How would it be were they to have seen My Paradise?' They say, 'And they ask protection of You.' He says, 'From what do they ask protection of Me?' They say, 'From Your Hellfire, O Lord.' He says 'Have they seen My Hellfire?' They say, 'No.' He says, 'How would it be were they to have seen it?' They say, 'And they ask Your forgiveness.' Then He says, 'I have forgiven them, and I have bestowed upon them what they have asked for. And I have granted them sanctuary from that from which they ask protection.' They say, 'O Lord, among them is a much sinning servant, who was merely passing by and sat down with them.' He says, 'To him also I have given forgiveness. He who sits with such people shall not suffer.' "

Within Sufism there is an understanding that when there is a *dhikr* circle, those within that circle are praising Allah, that when they repeat His Name and remember Him, the angels are present and protecting them. This is a real experience, which at times, if one continued the repetitions combined with various other movements, can enable one to attain a mystical state.

There was a sheikh who came to Istanbul. He was a wandering dervish. He went to the governing authority in charge of religious affairs and asked for a building to be used as a *tekke*.

"How many dervishes do you have?" the officials asked.

"I just have this one dervish," he said, "and myself."

They thought this odd, but there was an old rundown building, and they agreed to give it to him. He accepted, and with his one dervish, occupied the building. Very soon there was an enormous light coming from within this building. The sound of *dhikr* could be heard every night, and crowds of people attended. The light was great and bright.

The governing authorities in charge of *tekkes*, dervish prayer lodges, wanted to know what this man was doing to draw so many people to him. And what about this light that was reported coming from the old building, which the sheikh had now rebuilt. So they sent for him.

The officials said, "We are the educated ones, and we want to question you to make certain you are doing things correctly."

"All right."

"What is the meaning of *la ilaha illa Allah*?" they asked.

"Do you want the meaning as you understand it, or do you want the meaning as I understand it?"

"We know how we understand it. Tell us how you understand it."

"For this I need my one dervish, the one I brought with me the first time I came to this building."

They agreed, and sat down as he and his dervish began to make the *dhikr*. When he said, "*la ilaha*," his dervish disappeared. When he said, "*illa Allah*," he reappeared. When he said, "*la ilaha*," again, they both disappeared. When he said, "*illa Allah*," they reappeared.

The last time he said, *"la ilaha,"* the entire room disappeared. And when he said, *"illa Allah,"* everyone reappeared.

He turned to face the officials and said, "This is how I understand the *dhikr.*"

La ilaha, there is no God—if there is no God, then we do not exist. *Illa Allah*, but Allah. And if Allah exists, He has created us, and we appear.

Once an Abyssinian came to meet the Prophet. The presence of the Prophet Muhammad was so overpowering that this man standing before him began to sway back and forth. When the Prophet saw this, he also began to sway back and forth. This was the beginning of the swaying movement in the *dhikr*. Every movement has a meaning. When the Rufai or the Halveti put a skewer through their cheeks and there is no blood and no wound, it relates to the story of Zuleika and Joseph in Egypt. The maidens couldn't believe that she was so in love with Joseph. Zuleika warned them to wait until they saw him. He reflected the Beauty of Allah. They were all in the kitchen peeling and cutting vegetables when Joseph entered. When they saw him, they couldn't believe their eyes, and they kept on cutting vegetables, not feeling and not knowing that they were cutting their fingers.

Everything in the *dhikr* has a direct meaning and a reason. The reason underlying all the reasons is always to come closer to Allah. To remember Him. If we continuously say His Name, perhaps one day He will choose to repeat His Name through us. There are men who while doing *dhikr* have been transported from the Namer to the Named. We have to become like the boat of Noah, so that anyone who comes near us, anyone who touches us, can be helped.

THE TRAVELER'S DREAM

There is a *hadith* that states: "If my servant makes mention of Me to himself, I make mention of him to Myself; and if he makes mention of Me in an assembly, I make mention of him in an assembly better than it. And if he draws near to Me a hand's span, I draw near to him an arm's length."

We each have a personal relationship with Allah. When we say His Name, we come closer to Him. Allah is as close to us as our jugular vein. This is the vein in the side of the neck that carries blood from the head to the heart.

If Allah is far, if the journey seems too great a distance for us to travel, then we are carrying too much luggage. If that is the case, we should take inventory of ourselves. Maybe even close the shop of our lives for a couple of days and examine how each of us spends his time, emotions, energy, and money. If we feel that life is precious, that it is a gift of Allah who created us, then what do we do with this gift? How do we spend the time between prayers? What do we speak about? If you listen to most conversations, you will hear people talk about what a great dinner or lunch they had at this restaurant. It seems funny, but it's true and sad. In our own time each one of us should take an inventory of the shop that is ourself. What are the things in this shop that are no longer useful? That we've outgrown? Look around your house, and you'll see clothes that you haven't worn in a year, yet you still keep them.

We do it with relationships, we do it with friendships. If we don't make them grow, we won't make them better. Yet we also don't discard them. We're stuck with all this luggage. We are attached to it. But how to get unattached? How to let go of this luggage that we know we no longer need. Whether it be too much television, too many useless conversations, too much external entertainment, or whatever, where is the meaning in our life?

While we're young, we never think this life will end. But it will. Yes, we have been given a free will to choose how to live in this life. We can either seek a way that tells us how to do it, that prescribes some recipes that work for us, or choose to ignore all these simple wisdoms and just haphazardly go through life.

At any rate, no matter how young we are, one day we will be older.

Once a king and his party were hunting in the desert. Somehow the king got separated from his party. Riding alone, he saw a bedouin tent in the distance. He kicked his horse and galloped toward the tent. He had been wandering for a long time in the hot desert, trying to find his men, and he was extremely thirsty. He announced himself, and an old woman came out of the tent.

"Get me a glass of water, I'm thirsty," the king ordered.

She said, "It's not easy to get you a glass of water in the desert."

"I'm a king."

"You may be a king in Baghdad, but you're not the king in this tent."

She brought out a glass of water and held it up to the king. "What will you give for this glass of water?" Before he had a chance to answer, she quickly added, "I don't mean gold, which you may think I want."

At that moment the king was thinking that the old woman wanted gold. Realizing that she had read his mind, the king concluded that she was no ordinary being.

He asked, "What is it that you want?"

She said, "How long have you been king?"

He answered, "Forty years."

"I'll take forty years from you," she said.

"Do you want the forty years that I've been king, or do you want the forty years that are to come?"

"You can keep the forty years that are to come," she said, "and I'll take the forty years that have passed."

As he looked back over those forty years, he realized that they were all encapsuled in the very second he was facing the woman. He reasoned: Indeed, she's really asking for nothing in return for the water. And then he said, "You can have those forty years."

She gave him the water and said, "If you don't have faith in Allah and don't treat your people better, the next forty years will be the same as those that have just passed."

When he finished the water, the tent and the woman disappeared. He concluded it had all been a dream. But at once he also realized he was no longer thirsty.

Each of us, when we take our inventory, can look at the twenty, twenty-five, thirty, thirty-five, or forty years that have passed, as times of joy and times of pain. They are all contained in this second right here and now. There is only this second.

If we don't have faith in Allah, if we don't repeat His Name, when we look back at our lives, it will be just a blink of an eye, a quick second, and gone.

The dervish associates with people who remind him of Allah . . . of the Beauty of Allah or of an aspect of Allah's attributes, remind him to wake up and remember Allah. Those are the people to be associated with. Everyone can be a teacher. Sometimes the best teachers are those who teach us what not to do. The drunk lying on the Bowery in a stupor is a message for those who want to see. The man who sees the drunk might understand the nature of drunkenness. He might also see how the man got to that state and even understand the effect that put him in the gutter. But that is all viewed from the outside. As for the drunken man, he is totally at one with his drunkenness. That is why in Sufism you'll often see: "Drink the wine of love in the tavern of the Sufi."

We can learn lessons from everyone. We can learn much from those who have come before us. All is temporary save Allah. What can last? Where are the Mesopotamians? Where are the Romans? Where is Pompeii? At one time the Romans ruled the known world.

When Alexander the Great was dying, he called his physicians to him. This man, the Greek who had conquered most of his world at a young age, pleaded with his physicians: "I will give you half my kingdom, half of the entire world, if any of you can prolong my life just long enough for me to see my mother again."

The physicians went off to the side to discuss it. Presently they came back and said, "Sire, even if you were to give your entire kingdom, no one can extend your life for even one breath longer than it is meant to be."

Hearing this verdict, he resigned himself to his fate and gave instructions that the next day, during his funeral procession, the coffin should remain open. And that his empty hands should be open, exposing his palms upward and hanging from the sides of the coffin in a supplicating gesture so that everyone could witness that Alexander the Great, the man who saw and conquered the known world, now left empty-handed.

What can we take with us? The only thing we can take with us are our good deeds.

The man who's lying in the street in a drunken stupor may at that moment imagine himself a king. He could be dreaming that he lives in a golden room attended by many servants, being honored by a great and royal feast. Indeed dreaming, only to wake up to reality.

There once was a traveler who was tired and dirty from the road, who upon arriving in Istanbul, headed for—as was the custom in those days—the *hammam*, the public bath. In those days you could also get a small amount of opium for not much money when you went to the *hammam*. He was a poor man. Nevertheless, he decided to treat himself to a piece of candy with opium in it. That's how it was sold. The attendants washed him, and when they were finished, he lay down to relax on the marble platform, a kind of bier. And there he lay in the quietness surrounded by steam.

After a while he heard noise of voices and shuffling. He looked around, and there by an archway he saw a man being guided into a room and being attended to with meticulous care by three men. He concluded that the man must be very important. In contrast, nobody had come to bathe him. He scrutinized the scene with great care and took particular notice that they had given the man one of the larger, more luxurious private rooms. In the old *hammam*s there were large public bathing rooms for the poorer people and private, more elaborate bathing facilities with individual attendants for the rich.

Soon the attendants left the man alone in his private and luxurious bathing cubicle. After a while, his curiosity somewhat aroused, the traveler decided to take a closer look at the man. Slowly he walked over and looked in. Astonished, he saw that the man and he looked exactly alike. It was like looking in a mirror. The man could have been his identical twin.

The man appeared to have fallen asleep. The poor traveler moved a little closer and nudged him. Cold! He nudged him again and again. Nothing. Then, upon closer examination, he realized that the man was dead. He thought: Who would know the difference? Why not? I look exactly like this man. He's obviously extremely wealthy. And I have nothing . . . .

The poor man changed places with the dead rich man, laid his body on the marble slab that he had occupied, and installed himself in the luxurious cubicle. When the attendants came back, they finished bathing him and after drying and dressing him in silk and satin, escorted him out into the hallway. They placed a huge fur coat on his shoulders. He softly caressed the silk and satin. As he reached into the pockets of his new clothes, he found gold and silver coins, which he distributed generously to all the people who had attended him.

Suddenly, from behind him, he heard a loud commotion. He saw the attendants dragging a cloth sack, and judging from the shape, he deduced it contained the body of the dead man. With a sigh of relief, he smiled inwardly, thinking that this could have been him.

Because he thought his voice would give him away, he decided it best to keep quiet. Not knowing what to do, how to act with these people, he let them escort him outside, and there, waiting for him, was a beautiful carriage. He got in. The driver snapped the whip, the horses made loud breathy noises, and the carriage rode off. He sat back and, wondering about it all, thought: Who am I? Well, I'll be patient, and then, because they're taking me to my home, maybe I'll know and understand more and be able to put a few things together.

They brought him to an enormous and beautiful house. It was like a palace. He thought, I must truly be a wealthy man. As they were talking, he soon realized he was a member of the government. After a little more talk he realized that he was none other than the sultan's vizier. Ah, but who?

Upon entering, the servant asked him, "Would you like to sleep in your private quarters or in the harem tonight?" He thought, I'd better sleep in my private quarters, because certainly the ladies will soon discover that I'm not who I'm supposed to be.

So he went into his private quarters, thinking and wondering how long this could last. It seemed wonderful. One of the servants came in and said, "The sultan is calling for you first thing in the morning." When the servant left, the man thought he was in trouble. Big trouble. Because certainly the sultan and the people at the palace would discover him. His punishment would be great—

indeed royal!

Later that night, he stuffed as many gold and silver coins in his pockets as he could and disappeared into the night. He ran and ran. . . until he came upon a cemetery.

Mosques sometimes have cemeteries attached to them and little rooms near the cemeteries. He made his way inside, found an empty casket, and decided to hide in it. He climbed inside and thought: I'll be safe here, who could look for me in a coffin?

No sooner had he made himself comfortable in the coffin than he heard voices. He lifted the lid and looked out. And there he saw three men who looked like thieves. They had just committed a big robbery. They had an enormous amount of loot and were distributing it among themselves right there in the middle of this room full of coffins. As he climbed out of the coffin to take a closer look, he made a sharp noise. One of the thieves looked over his way. He got frightened and ran, and they chased him. They chased him all around the mosque, up and down the minaret, and all over the grounds. They were going to kill him, he was convinced. They finally caught him. And just as they were about to kill him, they pushed him, and he fell onto a very hard and cold surface. He opened his eyes, rubbed the pain of his head, and saw that he was in the *hammam* on the floor, just under the marble platform where he had fallen asleep. And he realized that it had all been a dream.

If you don't know where you came from, and you don't know where you are, and you don't know where you are going, your life will continue to be a dream. Like the dream of this man who thought he was wealthy, who thought he was a vizier to the sultan.

Sometimes in life we witness or experience certain things that are best not talked about.

A man heard a knock at his door. He went and opened the door, and the man standing there on the threshold said, "This is a house of Allah. I'm a traveler. Please let me rest here."

111

The man said, "This is my house. You want the house of Allah? Go down to the mosque," he said, "that's the house of Allah! Don't bother me." He slammed the door.

The man went down the road, knocked on another door. An elderly woman came, and he said, "I'm a traveler, and I'm tired and hungry."

She said, "Please come in. I don't have much to give you. There's a little left over from dinner you can have. There's a tiny room upstairs, and you're welcome to spend the night."

He thanked her, went upstairs and slept. In the morning when he came down, she had prepared hot milk and tea. They sat at the table and talked. He expressed his gratitude and thankfulness. And she said, "No, not at all, it's our duty to help those in need."

He smiled back and said, "Well, I'm the Devil." She became pale, stepped back, and got very frightened. He said, "Don't be frightened. I wouldn't harm you. You've helped me. But I would like a favor of you, if you don't mind."

She said, "Well, okay. Whatever you like."

He said, "I'm going to change myself into a donkey, then I would like you to take me to the marketplace and to sell me for nine pieces of gold. Only I'll indicate to you the person that you are to sell me to."

She said, "All right."

He changed himself into the most beautiful donkey. She led him to the marketplace, which was very crowded. They walked around, and the Devil as donkey edged his way through people until he came to the man who was to buy the donkey. It was the man who had refused him lodging the night before.

The woman offered the donkey. He thought it was a beautiful donkey and asked, "How much?"

"Nine pieces of gold."

"That's a lot for a donkey."

After a few more exchanges and with the help of the donkey,

she seemed to convince him that it was indeed a good buy.

So he bought the donkey for nine pieces of gold. He got on the donkey's back and rode him pompously through the marketplace. He stopped to pick up some hay and offered it to his expensive donkey. The donkey refused the hay.

Well, maybe the donkey's thirsty, he thought. It's a hot day. He saw a water fountain. The kind where you press a button and the water comes out from a tiny spout. He went to get some water for the donkey and pressed the button. As he released it, the donkey disappeared right into the little spout of the water fountain.

He looked in and saw the donkey's ears standing straight up forming a kind of V-shape and waving. He looked in again to make sure that this was really what he was seeing, and he could see the eye of the donkey and the ears waving. The donkey was just smiling at him.

A crowd had gathered around him. Here was this man looking inside a waterspout and begging someone to come out, saying, "I just paid so much money for you; don't just wave your ears at me. Come on out." A crowd gathered, and soon the police came and asked, "What is it? What's the matter with you?"

"Well, my donkey was just here, and he disappeared as I got him some water. He's right inside the spout of that water fountain," the man insisted.

The police looked, as did some bystanders, but no one saw anything. Still the man insisted.

They took him to the madhouse. They assigned him a room in the main ward, and there, day after day, he kept insisting that his donkey was inside the water fountain. They put him in a strait-jacket, and after some time a good friend of his came to visit.

"Listen, this may be something that actually happened," the friend advised, "but as long as you tell these people this story, they're never going to let you out of here. You've got to change your story. It's your only chance of being released."

"I'll try it. Anything. I don't want to stay here."

The next day the doctor came and asked him, "How are you?"

He answered, "I'm fine."

"And the donkey?" the doctor asked.

"What donkey?"

"Well, you know, you said that your donkey jumped into the spout of the water fountain."

"Oh, that. Well, doctor, I had taken some medicine, and I think I must have started hallucinating."

The next day he told the doctor the same story, and he decided he could release him. Attendants took the strait-jacket off and released him. He went right to the water fountain. He looked into the water spout, and there he saw the eye of the donkey, and the donkey's ears were waving at him.

He said to the donkey, "You know you're in there, and I know you're in there, but if I tell anyone else that you're in there, they're going to put me in a strait-jacket again."

There are some things you see in life and don't speak about. Some things can remain a secret. A secret is something that only exists between two people, and sometimes only with yourself.

In Islam, when we begin a conversation or greet someone, we say *as-salaam aleykum*, peace and blessings be upon you, first.

The year before last, I was in Madinah. On the plane going there, I told my traveling companion there was a man whom I had met four years earlier in Madinah whom I would like to see again. His name was Abdullah Faraj, and he was one of the few living descendants of the Ansar, the people who greeted the Prophet Muhammad when he was driven from Makkah to Madinah. That year Abdullah Faraj came to a small *dhikr* we had in Madinah, and he sang. His voice was beautiful. At one time he was the *muezzin*, the man who chants the call to prayer, at the Prophet's mosque in Madinah.

Before we left to go on *umra*, the small pilgrimage, I called some

114

friends in Istanbul and asked, "How am I going to find Abdullah Faraj?" They said, "Just ask anybody in the mosque. Everybody knows him."

Arriving at the mosque, we saw that most of the people were visitors like us. We questioned a few men about the whereabouts of Abdullah Faraj, and nobody knew. We asked everyone we met. No one knew him. This went on for days.

The day before leaving, we had to pick up my traveling companion's parents at the bus station. We didn't know where that was. So we stopped anyone on the way, from the street cleaner to the shopkeepers, saying, "*as-salaam aleykum*, can you tell us where the bus station is?"

After questioning several people and getting a lot of confusing gestures indicating many directions, we came to a crossing where workers were building a tunnel. It was dusty, and the desert sand was blowing up into our faces. I led my companion and said, "Let's go across the street." We were now facing a building with a long bench along one side of it, where three men were having tea.

My companion, whose name was Hussein and who spoke Arabic, faced them and asked, "Where is the bus station?"

One of the men looked at him and said, "Don't you say *as-salaam aleykum* first?"

Hussein said, "Oh, I'm terribly sorry."

This man then proceeded to give us a lecture on the text that nothing is ever said, no directions are ever asked for, and no conversation is ever begun before one says *as-salaam aleykum*. He went on and on, and Hussein said, "I'm terribly sorry. Please forgive us. My name is Hussein, this is Shemsuddin."

We moved closer to the men, and I asked this one man, "What is your name, sir?"

He said, "I'm one of the few living descendants of the Ansar. My name is Abdullah Faraj."

Hussein and I looked at each other, and I repeated, "What did

115

you say your name was, sir?"

He said, "Abdullah Faraj."

And I said, "*Alhamdulillah!*"

I told him the name of my sheikh in Istanbul.

He said, "*Halvatiyya, Halvatiyya,*" and we embraced each other. He invited us to sit down and gave us tea.

"This was the wish of Allah," he began again. "It was from Allah that you did not say *as-salaam-aleykum*, because if you had said *as-salaam-aleykum*, I would have said *wa-aleykum-as-salaam*, the bus station is over there. There's a frontier between." With his hand he indicated the green dome above where the Prophet lies. "From there to here"– he placed his hand to his heart, meaning there was a direct line –"there's a barrier, a frontier. Everyone can pass through this barrier, but not everyone can stop here. Allah wanted you to stop here, because we had to have this conversation and were meant to meet. So He didn't let you say *as-salaam aleykum.*"

He invited us to come and have tea with him the following day. When we arrived, he was making little glass-framed containers. They were about three inches high, and glued at the edges. He didn't care if they were exact or matched perfectly. Inside each one of them was a layer of clay with what looked like little bones mixed with pieces of clay.

Hussein asked him what he was doing. He had several of these glass containers lined up, and he was placing them in the back of a car.

"I'll tell you when I'm finished," Abdullah Faraj said. We drank the tea he had given us. When we finished, he had finished what he was doing. Then he faced us and said, "When I heard they were building this tunnel, between where I'm sitting, which is right under the mosque of Ali, and there, which is the place of the tomb of the Prophet, I surmised that they would have to dig and touch the exact earth that the Prophet walked upon. So that night I went and made what's called an *istahara.*" *Istahara* is the reciting of several different

116

chapters from the Quran, a form of prayer in which one asks guidance of Allah, and an answer comes through a dream or by some other means.

"That night I made an *istahara*," Abdullah Faraj said. "And in my sleep an old man appeared in my dream. This old man told me to go to a particular place, which was just along the path where the Prophet walked to do his afternoon prayer at the mosque of Omar. It was also a watering place where he stopped to drink and a place where sheep drank. This man said to me that if I dug one meter and thirty-two centimeters down in this place, I'd have the exact earth that the Prophet walked upon."

That very same night, before early morning prayer when it was still dark, Abdullah Faraj went out with a flashlight and a shovel to the place indicated in his dream and started digging. He measured it exactly one meter and thirty-two centimeters. There he found chips of sheep bone and pieces of clay pots. He took a large sampling of the earth and gave it to a chemist to analyze, not telling him where he got it. He asked the chemist for the approximate dates to determine the age of this earth. And indeed the chemist dated it at the time the Prophet was living in Madinah.

Abdullah Faraj then took us to his home, and gave us each a little packet which he had prepared before we got there. Each packet contained a small block of the earth that the Prophet walked upon. It was his gift to us.

That was a year ago last March. This small block of earth still gives off the scent of roses.

Then he sang for us. This made our visit complete. The next day we left Madinah.

In Makkah and Madinah there are wonderful and incredible beings who are disguised. You only see them if they choose to reveal themselves to you. We had many similar experiences. And *Insha' Allah*, if you go, you will also experience Makkah and Madinah.

117

REMEMBER YOUR DEATH

 One night, while walking the countryside in upstate New York, we saw something that Hussein had never seen before. Something quite familiar in the West. It was a firefly. He saw these lights flickering in the trees, and said, "By Allah, what is that?"

"Oh, that's a firefly."

"You mean that it lights up? How does it light up? Why does it light up?" Hussein, who is from Egypt, had never seen a firefly before.

Let's think about fireflies. It's the male firefly that lights up to attract the female. It's interesting because one wonders: Does the firefly feel any different when it has light passing through it? Or when it doesn't? Is there a difference in its being? Because it's probably very similar to when we experience a sensation of light flowing in us. That light has been touched in us and touched our hearts in such a way that we feel different. And someone could say, there is a *nur*, a light, coming from you.

This is the Light of Allah. The *Nur, Nur al-Muhammadi*, the *Nur a-Nur*. The Light of the Divine Light. And there are times within each of us that we can see it in one another, even see it in ourselves. We come to a sheikh, with all the wiring. It's as if Allah has placed all the wiring, but we can't find the switch. The sheikh helps us find the switch. Maybe he might even turn it on. But the light bulb is too dusty. The light doesn't really come out. But we feel a little different. At the same time that he turns the switch, he cleans the light bulb a little. A pinhole of light seems to come out. And you feel different. That pinhole of light can also be recognized by other people. Some may even comment, saying that you look different . . . you look very good, there's a light coming from you. Our job is to clean the rest of the light bulb.

The bear likes honey. And the bear will go after honey, no matter what. The bear will stick its paw in a beehive to get the honey. The bees will sting him continually. They will sting his paw, his arm, his body, and there will be swellings all over his face, but he will continue to go after the honey. No matter how much pain he has, no matter how many stings, he will not give up his desire for the honey. The intelligent bear, though, will pick up the beehive and throw it in the river. The bees, fearing they'll drown, will all fly away from the beehive. And when they've all gone, the intelligent bear will pick up the beehive and eat all the honey.

The world is like the stinging bees. We continually go after things that cause pain, and we get stung constantly. But isn't the sting of the world worth the honey of Allah? The intelligent person accepts the pain but doesn't nourish it. He doesn't give it a room in his house. If you continue to nourish the pain or loneliness or anger that you have, eventually you will have to give it a room in your house. It will then occupy a space within you.

The Sufis use the broom of *la*, of no, to sweep out these things from the heart. Sufis live according to the conditions, precepts, and conduct that were brought to them by the Prophet Muhammad. And all these can be found in the *Hadith*, Traditions of the Prophet.

If you allow room in your house for sorrow, laziness, and deceit, these will eventually take over your life, and it will be more difficult to find space for joy, happiness, and bliss.

So we attempt to clean our house of everything that is not Allah. With this broom of *la*, this broom of no. The broom of not giving in to our desires and lusts. The broom of the moment of knowing something is not good for us, to say no. To be protected by the cloak of faith, a robe woven by the Names and Attributes of Allah.

120

This robe is the *tawhid*, the *dhikr*. *Tawhid* is the phrase of Unity.

La ilaha illa Allah, there is no God but Allah, is a protective cloak. Faith is a gift that protects us.

Mevlana Jelalludin Rumi tells us that the grace of Allah bestows a throat on all things. The earth has a throat, and it drinks the water that's sent from the sky and becomes nourished, and in turn it gives off plants and herbs. Animals have a throat to eat these plants and herbs and to be nourished by them. Man has a throat, and he eats the animals. The question has been asked about Sufis eating meat. My sheikh has said to people who have asked him this, "When I eat a sheep, then I make that sheep a dervish. So I have bettered his level."

After the animal is food for man, eventually man disappears and goes into the earth, and the cycle continues. The faith that Allah has given us as a gift is a throat that consumes all the vanities and fancies of man. It's like the staff of Moses that ate the snake of the pharaoh.

Within us we have the equivalent of the staff of Moses. We have a faith that can devour the pharaoh's snake within us.

Moses was in the field one day, and Allah said to him, "What is it that you have in your hand?"

"A staff."

"And what do you do with this staff?"

Now Allah didn't have to ask this of Moses, of course. Allah would know, for He knows all. But He asked this of Moses so that their conversation can be repeated, and we can learn from it today. When He asked, "And what do you do with that staff?" Moses said, "I lean on it. And sometimes I use it to separate my sheep and keep them in line. Also I knock down leaves from trees so that my sheep will have some food."

Allah said, "Throw the staff to the ground."

He did, and the staff turned into a snake.

Then Allah said, "Pick up the snake."

And Moses picked up the snake.

This story could end right here, and this is the lesson: submission to Allah. Even with the fear that the snake could kill him, Moses' submission to Allah was greater than his fear of death.

He was told to throw the snake down, and he did, and it turned back into a staff. The real lesson for us is that if we lean on anything other than Allah, it could turn into a snake.

Then Allah said to Moses, "Place your hand on your heart," and he did. When he removed his hand, he saw written in the palm of his hand in *Nur*, Divine Light, the Name of Allah. Which signified that his heart had His Name engraved upon it. When one's heart becomes pure, then the sign of Allah is written upon our being.

There was a man who wanted a tattoo. He heard of a village high in the mountains where they had a famous tattoo artist. He went to the village and approached the old artist. He told him he wanted a tattoo.

The artist said, "Why do you want this tattoo? And what is it that you want tattooed?"

"I want a lion tattooed on my back," he said. "You see how big I am?" He was a huge man. "When I'm working in the fields and have my shirt off, that lion will show people for miles around that I'm there."

The artist sat him down, took out his needles, and began to tattoo his back. No sooner had the needle pierced his skin, than the man screamed, "Ouch! What part of the lion are you working on?"

"I'm working on the ear."

"Well, let it be a lion without an ear."

And so the artist began again, and the man screamed again, and writhing in pain he said, "What part of the lion are you working on now?"

"I'm working on the tail."

"Look, let it be a lion without a tail."

And again the artist began to give him what he wanted, and again the pain made him scream and he asked, "Now what part of the lion are you working on?"

"I'm working on the lion's mane."

"Let's make a lion without a mane."

At this, the old artist kicked him off the chair. "Look, what you want is the pleasure of the result, and you don't want to go through the pain of getting there."

We want the pleasure of being close to Allah. But we don't want to go through the process of getting there. We want to love Allah without loving His Creation. We want Allah to accept our love when we don't love those He's created. If we want to know Allah, we can know Him through His Creation.

How can we light the torch of faith in our hearts? With inspiration. We can make no action without its being preceded by inspiration. If we have an inspiration, it leads to a desire, and that desire will create an action. And how are we inspired? Obviously we're not inspired by a life vicariously lived while attached to video screens. We are involved with too much television and too much useless conversation. Too much involvement with who won a baseball game. I'm not saying you can't be interested in those things and even partake of them. But if they take over your life, it leaves no time to do real work.

We can be inspired by reading the holy books sent down by Allah and by reading the books of the Masters. We can become inspired by those around us who remind us of Allah. Sometimes, when I'm walking down the street with some of the elder dervishes, we may not even be talking, or if we are talking, it's not important, and invariably one of them, a man who has been my teacher, will say, "We're walking from here to there. Let's not waste this time. Let's talk about something important to both of us."

Now, how often do we find ourselves in our car, or walking down a street with a friend, and we allow precious time to slip away. We don't remind each other of Allah enough.

This is a letter written by a man Yahya to his son Faisal. It was written in A.D. 956. He said:

> My dear son,
>   May God keep thee safe and give me joy of thee. The Prince of the Faithful has learned with displeasure that hunting and amusements leave thee no time to attend to public affairs. Thou shouldst return to what will do thee more honor, for a man's good or bad habits are the only means whereby his contemporaries know him. Farewell.

And at the foot of the letter he added these verses:

> Seek glory all day long,
> No effort spare
> And patiently the Loved One's absence bear.
> But when the shades of night advancing slow,
> Over every vice a veil of darkness grow.
> Beguile the hours with all thy heart's delight,
> The day of prudent men begins at night.
> Many there be esteemed of life austere,
> Who nightly enter on a strange career.
> Night over them keeps her sable curtain drawn
> And merrily they pass from eve to dawn.
> Who but a fool his pleasures would expose
> To spying rivals and censorial foes?

The university of the dervish is the night. The dervish prays through the night. He sleeps little, eats little, and talks little. These are his protections. Through the night he prays to Allah. It is said that at certain times of night, Allah listens to all that His servants ask.

A dervish poet once wrote: "Associate with such a person whose sight wakes up the remembrance of God in you. And who does not instruct by words but by his example makes you perfect in your spiritual practice."

One day Jesus was walking by a field where there were a number of sheep. He went over to one of them and whispered in its ear, then continued on his way.

Several days passed. Once again he came walking by that same field. When he saw that the sheep he had spoken to had grown pale and thin, he was concerned. He went to the shepherd and asked about this sheep.

The shepherd, who did not recognize him as the man who had been there a few days before, said, "A man passed by this field a few days ago, and whispered something into the ear of that sheep, and from that moment, the sheep has not eaten or drunk anything." He paused and added, " I wonder what that man could have said to him."

What Jesus said to that sheep was, "There is death."

There is death so affected the sheep that he stopped eating. How does it affect us to know and understand that there is death? This body that we know and are familiar with and are so attached to will stop existing one day. What preparations are we making in order to avoid decay?

Another day, Jesus was walking along the road, and he came upon a man who was carrying a sack containing several loaves of bread. Jesus and the man greeted one another and walked down the road together. Jesus could not see the loaves, and as they walked, Jesus asked him, "How many loaves of bread do you have?"

The man, seeing that Jesus had no loaves of bread, said, "I have one."

They walked a way further and came upon a river. Jesus touched the river with his staff and it parted, making way for a dry path. They crossed the path to the other side and continued over the road. Again Jesus asked the man, "How many loaves of bread do you have?"

"One," he answered.

The man had witnessed a miracle, and his answer was still the same. They continued walking, and further along the road several men were carrying a coffin. In the Name of Allah, Jesus revived the dead man. They walked on, and again Jesus asked, "How many loaves of bread do you have?"

And again, the man answered, "I have one, one loaf."

They soon came upon a city. They were tired and rested by the side of the road. At a certain point, Jesus disappeared, leaving his staff against a tree. The king had a very sick daughter, and when he heard of Jesus' deeds, he dispatched his emissaries to bring Jesus to heal his daughter. The emissaries came and mistook the man sitting next to the staff of Jesus for Jesus.

"Are you Jesus? The king would like to see you."

"Yes, of course."

They took him back to the palace, and placed him before the girl. He touched the sick girl with the staff of Jesus, and she died. He was thrown into prison.

When Jesus heard of this, he came and, in the Name of Allah, revived the dead girl. Jesus asked the king to forgive the man for his mistake. The king forgave and released him. Soon they were on the road again, and Jesus asked him, "How many loaves of bread do you have?"

"One."

They came to five huge boulders, all made of pure gold, and Jesus said, "Here are boulders made of gold. Let's divide them. We'll divide them in the proportion of how many loaves of bread we each have."

The man quickly said, "I have three loaves."

Jesus turned to him and said, "You witnessed three miracles of Allah. You lied about how many loaves of bread you had. And for the gold of the world you would tell the truth. We cannot travel together any longer." Having said this, Jesus went on alone.

The man went from boulder to boulder, trying to move each one, trying to figure out how he could get them back to his village.

126

Finally he realized he couldn't budge even one of them. Presently two men arrived. They were bandits. They decided to become his partners. They said, "Look, the three of us together can find a way of moving the boulders. And we'll share the gold."

"All right," he said, and he added, "My village is closest to here."

"That's good," they agreed. "Go to your village and bring back a large cart. We'll load the boulders onto the cart, and then we'll take it to the village, and we'll share the gold."

And so the man ran off to his village. The two bandits talked among themselves, and said, "Look, when he comes back with the cart, we'll kill him. Why do we need a partner? We can have all this gold for ourselves."

The man arrived at his house, harnessed a horse to a huge cart, and told his wife, "While I finish setting up this cart, you bake a pie and put poison in it." To himself, he went on: Why should I share this gold with those two bandits? I'll give them some of this delicious pie, and then they'll die. I'll have all the gold myself.

The wife baked a delicious-looking pie and he placed it in the cart. He then rode back to the five boulders of gold. The bandits were ready and waiting for him when he got off the cart. They jumped him and with long knives stabbed him to death. They then proceeded to load the gold onto the cart. After they were finished, they saw the pie. They thought: We're hungry, we've worked up a good appetite from all this hard work. So they ate the pie, and the poison in it killed them.

If you spend your life going after the gold of this world, you will have neither the gold nor yourself.

There was a *hoja*, a teacher, of a very small village. Often in the East, villages have one *hoja*, one learned man, who acts as the *imam* and the teacher. And so it was that one day, after prayers, the *hoja* was giving a discourse in the mosque. At one point, he was interrupted by a question.

He said, "I don't know the answer," and he continued the

discourse. Soon, another man asked a question. He looked at him and said, "I don't know the answer to that either." Then somebody in the back yelled out, "*Hoja*, we're paying you all this money, and we ask you questions, and what do you say to us? I don't know the answer?"

"Brother," the *hoja* said, "you are paying me to tell you what I know. If you had to pay me to tell you what I don't know, this village would be impoverished."

There are two important things to remember in Sufism, and all the great sheikhs will tell you this. That is: Remember Allah; and remember your death. Death as a symbol and in actuality is a reminder that we're passing through this space, that this life, in the form as we know it, is finite. That all things we regard as precious, all things that we spend our time coveting and collecting, we will one day have to give them up.

It's important to be aware that one day you are going to die. If you are aware of this, then you are also aware of Allah as your Creator. Then you have achieved an awareness of death devoid of fear. Awareness that this life can be used as a preparation, a place to do work and prepare for the other life, which is promised in the Quran by Allah. One day, when we are placed in the grave, when none of our friends and loved ones can come with us, when none of our possessions can follow us, the only things that will be there to help us are our good actions.

The Prophet said: "Our Lord (glorified and exalted be He) descends each night to the earth's sky when there remains the final third of the night, and He says: Who is saying a prayer to Me that I may answer it? Who is asking something of Me that I may give it him? Who is asking forgiveness of Me that I may forgive him?"

If we continue to repeat the Name of Allah in the *dhikr* and remember Him, He will not forget us when we need Him.

The horse of death will come for everyone. For some when they are young, for others in middle age, for most when they are old—we don't know. But we do know that one day we will all be placed in the box that sums up our actions. We will have to account for these actions. If we can believe that Allah has created us and asked us to perform specific acts in preparation for this time, then we can learn the lessons of those who have come before us. Then we also have the possibility of not suffering through death. People die in different ways. There are some people who die very easily, with a smile, almost looking forward. While others suffer terribly.

It's not an escape from this earth, this world. I once saw an Arabic inscription on the tombstone of a Bektashi sheikh. It had his name, and underneath was written: *He has escaped.* But escaping does not mean a way out. Suicide is not allowed in Islam. In Islam we do not believe in reincarnation. We believe that one goes back to Allah, the Source. There is a process of time that is not measured in time as we know it.

It is important to know that Allah sees all of our actions, the good ones and the bad ones. An action can be good in one case and not in another.

There once was a man who was crossing the desert on horseback. He had to tie up his horse and go off on an errand. Looking around, he saw no place he could tie up his horse. He soon found a stick, which he planted in the ground and tied his horse to. He then walked off. When he came back, he untied his horse and thought: I'll leave the stick, so if another traveler comes after me, he will have a place to tie up his horse. He rode off. His intention was good.

Later that day, a man came walking by the spot where the stick had been planted, and he thought: I should pull this stick out of the ground, because if someone travels by night, he could bump into this stick and hurt himself. So he pulled it out and threw it down.

These were two opposite actions. Yet in the eyes of Allah, both were good actions.

129

In this life it is important to have awareness. Sometimes it is also good to be unaware. But it is terrible to be unaware of the existence of Allah. There are times when Allah has provided an unawareness that is beneficial to us. If a loved one dies, we suffer a terrible pain. If the arrow of this pain in our heart continued for a very long time, we could not live in this world. So Allah has placed an unawareness as a veil before us to ease the pain.

We don't know the time of our own death. This is a great gift from Allah. Because if we knew when we would die, we would stop building, we would stop working. We wouldn't place one stone on top of another. So unawareness in this case is a benefit.

THE DANCING BEAR

 In every dervish order there is a *silsila*, a chain of transmission. Each order is connected as in a large tree with many branches. As the early branches of a tree grow into many other branches, so do the chains of transmission weave and intersect with other chains, which all lead back to the Prophet. Sheikhs are usually given a *hirka*, mantle of honor and investiture, from their sheikh. It was the custom in many of the early dervish orders that the chain of spiritual guidance went from father to son. But if the son was not worthy, another person was given the honor. A sheikh never gave the mantle of leadership to his son unless he was truly worthy of that position.

Sheikhs have *khalifas*. *Khalifas* are deputies who have been given *ijaza*, a license to teach. *Ijaza* is also a parchment-like scroll inscribed with the entire lineage of the order, going all the way back to the Prophet Muhammad, and the last name on it is the new *khalifa*. It authenticates your connection to a true line of transmission and is a license from your sheikh allowing you to teach.

There are some *ijaza* that just say: This person has passed through a particular training, having reached a certain level, and is authorized to teach under certain circumstances that are up to the discretion of the sheikh. In the Mevlevi order, the highest of the sheikhs, the *pir*, is Mevlana Jelalludin Rumi. All other Mevlevi sheikhs are called *dedes*—men who have gone through the arduous *chille*, a retreat, which consists of a thousand and one days.

Every individual honored with *khalifa* and *ijaza* is also given specific instructions and spiritual prescriptions, which vary from

131

one order to the next. In the Halveti-Jerrahi Order, for instance, to become the sheikh, you have to go through the practice of reciting twenty-eight specific Names of Allah, repeating every one of the twenty-eight a hundred thousand times. It can take years to complete the task.

Sometimes, a sheikh is chosen or confirmed by means of a dream. Sheikh Muzaffer Efendi, the last grand sheikh of the Halveti-Jerrahi Order, was confirmed by a dream. The grand sheikh before Sheikh Muzaffer was Fahreddin Efendi. It was his intention that Muzaffer Efendi become the grand sheikh after he had passed away. But when that time came, there were some who did not readily accept Muzaffer Efendi because they felt that they had been with the order longer and had achieved a higher spiritual station. It was agreed, as is the custom, that all the *khalifas*, the deputies of the order, would go and make an *istahara*, a special prayer, and ask about the correctness of the choice and see if an answer could be revealed in a dream. The next Thursday night, the dervishes met again. Before anyone spoke, the man who wanted to be sheikh got up and said, "Wait! I've been very insistent about being the sheikh. But I had a dream last night. And in this dream, I saw Pir Nureddin Jerrahi place the *taj*, the golden turban, the sheikh's crown, upon Muzaffer Efendi's head. I now relinquish all expectations of being in that position. And I am the first to say that Muzaffer Efendi should be the sheikh, and even if it rained rocks, I would insist upon that."

There are a number of different ways to become a sheikh. But the selection is never haphazard.

The man who does not see all things from six sides is like a bear dancing to no purpose. This also relates to how we look at our relationships, our activities, and our work in life. And only then can we introduce seeing and hearing something through the ears and eyes of our heart. If we can attune the voice in our hearts to hear the Name of Allah within our hearts, if when we sleep, we can sleep with our hearts awake, our lives will change. A refinement will enter.

Words express what's in your heart. Many times you'll see the dervish make a gesture of putting his hand to his mouth and then to his heart. It means what is in my mouth is in my heart, and I will not say anything that is not in my heart.

A sheikh once said, If you plant peppers you cannot expect sugarcane. What you plant within the seedbed of your body is what will grow. You may not even reap what you sow within your lifetime but in another life. This life is a preparation.

Shibli was a great Sufi and a high-ranking member of the royal court. He was born into a distinguished and noble family; his mother was a renowned physician. When Shibli sought Truth, he placed himself in the hands of the enlightened Sheikh Hazrati al-Junayd of Baghdad. He was first put to work in the *tekke* cleaning the place of ablution. His mother felt sorry for her young son. He was such a sensitive boy and was given such harsh duty. So she brought twenty slaves to Hazrati Junayd and said, "Here, I've given you twenty slaves to work in my son's place. Can't they do the work?"

"You are a physician," al-Junayd said to her. "If your son had an ailment with his gallbladder, should I give the medicine to the slave?"

In the dervish order, the sheikh is the doctor who prescribes the medicine that each of us needs. My medicine can't be taken by you, and your medicine can't be taken by me.

Medicine is usually prescribed in specific quantities to be taken at a specific time. If you take all the medicine at once, it will not make you better. Most probably, it will make you sick. The same applies to any spiritual path. If you attempt to do all of the exercises that the sheikh prescribes too soon and all at one time, you may cause yourself more harm than good. This is important, because our immediate tendency is to want to do it all at once.

It's far better to follow a prescribed practice of 70,000 *tawhid, la ilaha illa Allah*, in sets of a thousand per day, than all 70,000 in one day.

A warrior was walking in a field when he saw a man sleeping under a tree. He was seated with his head cocked back against the trunk and his mouth agape. A large black snake was hanging from a branch just above him.

The warrior ran toward the sleeping man. He was too late. Just as he approached the man, the snake slithered down into his body, using the wide open mouth as a gate.

The warrior woke the man and with sword in hand chased him in circles about the field. The man was perplexed. His fear kept him ahead of the warrior. In between gasps he would ask what he might have done to anger the man that he would chase him.

There were apple trees in the field, and the warrior stopped the man only long enough to force him to eat large amounts of the rotten apples which had fallen to the ground. Again he would chase him, and again he would stop and force the man to stuff himself with rotten apples, until finally the man vomited all the rotten apples and the black snake.

Upon seeing the snake, the man was horrified. The warrior told him that, if he had known there was a black snake in him, he would have been so terrified that he might have died of fright. What happened was the only way to deal with the snake.

The man, who had at first thought that he was being chased by an enemy, realized that the warrior was his friend.

The sheikhs are sometimes like this. They ask us to do things that we don't always understand in order to have us be rid of a black snake that we may not even know resides within us.

We don't know what to do with our leisure; it has become an affliction. For the dervish, the chief means of training the *nafs*, the ego, are fasting and little sleep. We should sleep little, eat little, and talk little. He who truly fasts is one who keeps his mind free from the poisoned food of base suggestions. It's not simply not eating at a prescribed time.

Allah created the Prophet Adam from a mixture of water and earth. He created him out of this clay. For forty years, He kneaded this clay. Thirty-nine of those years were filled with pain. There was only one year of joy, of bliss, as He kneaded this clay into the shape of a human being.

Allah allowed Adam to perceive that his physical body was made of mud so that he would never forget that he was created only by the Will of Allah. And that nothing can be changed without the Will of Allah.

There once was a tyrant in a small village near the mountain where Moses spoke with Allah. A villager came to Moses and said, "O Moses, the next time you go to speak to Allah, could you please find out how long this tyrant is to live."

That was an acceptable question. He didn't ask, can Allah destroy the tyrant? It is acceptable to want to know how long one is going to be oppressed, how long there will be pain, how long there will be difficulty. He simply wanted to know how long this tyrant, who was constantly inflicting misery on his village, would live. As Moses walked a little further along the mountain road, the wife of this man also came to him, and said, "When you go to speak to Allah, would you please ask how long this tyrant will be here in this village tyrannizing us?" As Moses got closer to the mountain, the young son of this couple ran to him and said, "O Moses, when you speak to Allah, would you please ask Him how long this terrible tyrant will be here in our village? And how long will he live?"

Moses finally reached the mountain and made his way up to speak to Allah. When he came into the presence of Allah, he asked: "O Allah, there's a tyrant who is brutalizing this entire village. How long will he live?" And Allah answered, "This tyrant will live for three hundred more years."

135

Moses came down from the mountain, and the man ran over to him and asked, "Did you ask Allah?"

"Yes."

"How long is this tyrant going to be here?"

"Allah said three hundred years."

The man responded with, "There is no strength and no power except with Allah."

And as Moses walked back toward the village, the woman ran over to him and asked, "Did you ask Allah this question?"

He said, "Yes."

And she said, "How long is this tyrant going to live?"

And Moses answered, "Allah says for three hundred years."

She said, "There is no strength and no power except with Allah."

The young son then ran over to Moses and asked the same question, "Did you ask what I asked you of Allah?"

And Moses said, "Yes."

Then he asked, "What did Allah say? How long will this man tyrannize us?"

Moses said, "Allah said he will live for three hundred more years."

And the boy said, "There is no strength and no power except with Allah."

And as that last word left the young boy's lips, a terrible screaming was heard coming from the house of the tyrant. Then his family came running out saying that the tyrant had died just at that moment.

Moses was confused. He turned his being upward and said, "Allah, You said that this man would live three hundred more years, and I've come and told the people. If I am a prophet of Yours and I tell the people what You have told me, they won't believe in me any longer if something changes like that."

Allah said: "It is not for you to question Me. But when you came and asked that question, indeed that man was to live three hundred more years. But when you went down and the man asked you how long he would live and then said, There is no strength and no power except with Allah, I took a hundred years off the tyrant's life. And when the woman said the same, I took another hundred years. And when the young boy was told that he would live three hundred years and said to you, There is no strength and no power except with Allah, I immediately sent the Angel of Death to him." Nothing can change without the Will of Allah.

Sufism is the means of finding joy in the heart when afflictions come. Each one of us suffers afflictions in one way or another. The lighted candle is like a true Sufi. It gets up at night with a light-filled face, pale countenance, a burning heart, weeping eye, and is wakeful. The dervish who sleeps little and prays a lot to Allah finds that the sleep he thought he needed has become unnecessary. And the Darknesses from within have been removed and replaced by Light.

There were two horsemen riding across the desert. One was blind, and he was riding several feet behind his friend when he dropped his whip. He stopped, dismounted and, feeling the ground, searched for his whip. His hand came upon the whip. But something felt different. It was much longer and felt shiny and slicker. He thought: This is probably a much more beautiful whip than mine. He picked it up and climbed back on his horse and rode off after his friend, and they both rode on across the sand.

Midday wore on into afternoon, and when his friend looked back and saw, he said, "My friend, throw away what you have in your hand. It's a snake!"

The blind one said, "No, no! You just want this beautiful whip. I lost my whip a little way earlier, and when I went looking for it, I found this one. I can feel it's far more beautiful than the one I had. You're just telling me to throw it away so you can go and get it for yourself."

"Trust me, my friend, it's a snake."

"No, I know it's not a snake. It's a whip."

137

Now the hot midday desert sun had awakened the snake who had been sleeping in the cool shade of morning. It bit the blind man and killed him.

We have to listen to those who have a greater understanding of life when they tell us how to live. If not, often our choices can turn into a snake and even sometimes kill us.

The ones who do not learn from the lessons of others become lessons for others.

Our rope to Allah is prayer. To love your wife is a prayer . . . it makes a heart feel good.

To help humanity is prayer.

To help the poor is the prayer of money.

To prostrate oneself before Allah is the prayer of the body.

To say *la ilaha illa Allah* is the prayer of the mouth.

To love Allah is the prayer of the heart.

To look and see lessons in everything is the prayer of the eye.

To listen only to the truth and act accordingly is the prayer of the ear.

As long as you have faith in your heart, whatever you do is prayer.

Prayer will neutralize the masks you have worn and the poisons you have taken to get you through life.

Work as if you will live forever and pray as if you will die tomorrow.

I offer the following pages as a gift to all parents and children. It is the beautiful letter written by Imam Ali, the son-in-law of the Prophet Muhammad, to his son at the end of his life.

Ali, while only a boy, was one of the first to accept Islam and was so loved by the Prophet that he gave his daughter Fatimah to him in marriage.

This letter is a selection from the *Nahjul Balagha* by Imam Ali. Here is a practical teaching. This is how to live a life.

LETTER TO MY SON
BY IMAM ALI

 These advices are from a father, who realizes the mortality of life, who is getting old, who has patiently borne reverses and calamities, who hates inordinate desires and has overcome them, and who is shortly going to pass out of this world, to his son, who is young, who has the desire to lead the world to sober ways of thinking and better ways of life, a desire that is difficult to be achieved; a son who is mortal and is bound by nature to follow the steps of all mortals, is subject to ailments, is surrounded by misfortunes and calamities, has to face oppressions and tyrannies, has often to confront and sometimes to tolerate hypocrisy, deceit, guile, duplicity, and treason; a son who is to end his life in death, is to bear sufferings, is the heir to a person who is dead and gone, and who will end his life as a martyr to the animosity of his enemies.

After praise to Allah and the Prophet Muhammad (A.S.), let it be known to you that decay of health, passing away of time, and nearness of death have made me realize that I should give more thought to my future and to my people, advise them more, and spend more time in equipping them mentally to face this world. I felt that my own sons and my near ones have as much right to utilize my experiences and knowledge. All the ups and downs of life, all the realities, and all the truths about life and the hereafter that are known to me and others. I decided therefore to spend more time and to prepare you more for your future. This was neither selfishness nor self-esteem, nor any mental luxury of giving away advice, but instead the sincere desire to have you see the world as I found it, to look at the realities of life as I looked at them, and to do the right thing at the right time and in the right place as it should be done that made me write this down for you. You will not find here anything but truths and realities.

My dear son, you are part of my body and soul, and whenever I look at you, I feel as if I am looking at myself. If any calamity happens to you, I feel as if it has happened to me. Your death will make me feel as if it were my own death. Your affairs are like my own affairs. Therefore I commit this advice to paper. I want you to be attentive to it, and to guard it well. I may remain longer in your life or I may not, but I want this advice to remain with you.

First and foremost, my son, fear Allah. Be His obedient servant. Keep His thought always fresh in your mind. Be attached to and carefully guard the rope that connects you with Him. Can any other connection be stronger, more durable, and more lasting than this to command greater respect and consideration or to replace it?

Accept good advice and freshen your mind with it. Adopt piety and kill your inordinate desires with its help. Build your character with the help of sincere faith in religion and God. Subjugate your self-willed, obstinate, and refractory nature with the vision of death; see the mortality of life and of all that life holds dear; realize the actuality of misfortunes and adversities, the changes of circumstances and times, and study the histories of past people. See the ruined cities, the dilapidated palaces and decaying signs and relics of fallen empires and past nations. Then meditate over the activities of those people, over all they have done when they were alive and in power, what they have achieved, from where they started their careers, where, when, and how they were brought to an end, where are they now? What have they actually gained out of life and what was their contribution to human welfare? If you carefully ponder these problems, you will find that each one of those people has parted company with the others, and with all that they cherished and loved, for a solitary abode, alone and unattended, and you will also be like them.

Take care to provide well for your future abode. Do not lose eternal blessings for the sake of the pleasures of this mortal world.

Do not talk about things that you do not know. Do not speculate and pass judgment upon subjects that you are not in a position to form an opinion upon and are not called upon to do so. Give up when there is a possibility of your going astray. When there is danger of your wandering in the wilderness of ignorance and losing sight of the goal, it is better to give up the quest than to advance and face uncertain dangers and unforeseen risks.

Advise people to do good and to live virtuously, because you are fit to give such advice. Let your words and deeds teach the world lessons in how to abstain from wickedness and villainy. Try your best to keep away from those who indulge in vices and sins.

Fight, whenever required, to defend the cause of Allah. Do not be afraid that people will laugh at you, censure your action, or slander you. Fearlessly and boldly help truth and justice. Bear patiently the sufferings and face bravely the obstacles that come your way when you follow truth and try to uphold it. Adhere to the cause of truth and justice wherever you find it. Try to be well versed in Islamic law and theology and acquire a thorough knowledge of the canons of this religion.

Develop patience against sufferings, calamities, and adversities. This virtue of patience is one of the high values of morality and nobility of character, and is the best habit that one can develop. Trust in Allah and let your mind seek His protection in every calamity and suffering. Because you will thus entrust yourself and your affairs to the Best Trustee and to the Mightiest Guardian. Do not seek help and protection of anybody but Allah. Reserve your prayers, your requests, your solicitations, your supplications, and your entreaties for Him and Him alone. Because to grant, to give, to confer, and to bestow, as well as to withhold, to deprive, to refuse, and to debar lie in His and only in His Power. Ask as much of His

143

Favors and seek as much of His Guidance as you can.

Try to understand my advice, ponder it deeply, do not take it lightly and do not turn away from it. The best knowledge is that which benefits the listener. The knowledge that does not benefit anyone is useless and not worth learning or remembering.

My dear son, when I realized that I was getting old and when I felt that weakness and feebleness were gradually creeping over me, I hastened to advise you on the best ways of leading a noble, virtuous and useful life. I hated the idea that either death should overtake me before I could tell you all that I wanted to tell, or that my mental capacities, like my bodily strength, might fall prey to deterioration.

I convey all this knowledge to you, lest inordinate desires, temptations, and inducements start influencing you, lest adverse changes of times and circumstances drag you into their mire, lest I leave you like an unbroken and untrained colt. Because a young and fresh mind is like virgin soil, which allows things sown in it to grow verdantly and to bear luxuriously, I have therefore made use of early opportunities to educate and train you, before your mind loses its freshness, before it gets hardened or warped, before you start facing life unprepared for the encounter and before you are forced to use your decisions and discretions without gaining the advantages of the accumulated traditions, collected knowledge, and experiences of others. The advice and counsel that I give will save you from the worry of acquiring knowledge, gathering experiences, and soliciting others for advice. Now you can easily make use of all the knowledge men acquired with great care, trouble, and patience. Things that were hidden from them and that only experiments, experiences, and sufferings could bring to light are now made convenient and easily available to you through this advice.

My dear son! Though the span of my life is not as large as that of some others who have passed away before me, I took great care to study their lives. Assiduously I went through their activities. I

144

contemplated their deliberations and deeds. I studied their remains, relics, and ruins, and I pondered their lives so deeply that I felt as if I had lived and worked with them from the early ages of history down to our times, and I know what did them good and what brought harm to them. Sifting the good from the bad, I am concentrating within these pages the knowledge that I gathered. Through this advice I have tried to bring home to you the value of honest living and high thinking and the dangers of a vicious and sinful life, and I have covered and guarded every aspect of your life, as is my duty as a kind, considerate, and loving father.

From the very beginning, I wanted to help you develop a noble character and to prepare you for the life that you will have to lead, to train you to grow up to be a young man with a noble character, possessed of an open and honest mind and clear and precise knowledge of things around you. Originally, my desire was only to teach you the Holy Book thoroughly, to make you understand its intricacies, to impart to you the complete knowledge of His Orders and interdictions and not to leave you at the mercy of the knowledge of other people. But after having succeeded in this task, I felt nervous that I might leave you untrained and uneducated in these subjects that themselves are subject to so much confusion and so many contradictions. Subjects whose confusions have been made worse and confounded by selfish desires, warped minds, wicked ways of life, and sinful modes of thinking. Therefore I have noted down, in these lines, the basic principles of nobility, piety, truth, and justice. You may feel they are overbearing and harsh, but my desire is to arm you with this knowledge instead of leaving you unarmed to face the world where there is every danger of loss and damnation. As you are a noble, virtuous, and pious young man, I am sure you will receive Divine Guidance and succor. I am sure He will help you to achieve your aim in life. I want you to promise yourself to follow my advice carefully.

Remember, my son, the best of my advice is to tell you to fear

145

God, to concentrate, and to confine yourself to the performance of those duties that have been made incumbent upon you by Him and to follow in the footsteps of your ancestors and your pious and virtuous relatives. Verily they always carefully scanned their thoughts and deeds, as you must also try to do. This kind of deliberation made them take from life what was really the best and forsake that which was not made incumbent upon them. If your mind refuses to accept my advice and you persist in trying your own experiments, then you are at liberty to arrive at your own conclusions, but only after carefully studying the subject and after acquiring the knowledge necessary for such decisions. You must not allow uncertainties and doubts to poison your mind and skepticism or irrational likes and dislikes to affect your views. Remember that, before you start deliberating over a problem, seek guidance from the Lord and beseech Him to give you a lead in the right direction, avoid confusion in your ideas, and do not let disbelief about truth of the teachings of religion take hold of your mind, because one will lead you toward agnosticism and the other toward errors and sins. When you are thus prepared to solve any problem and you are sure that you possess a clear mind, a sincere and firm desire to reach the truth, to say the correct thing, and to do the correct deed, then carefully go through the advice that I am leaving you. If your mind is not as clear and free from doubts and skepticism as you wish it to be, then you will be wandering in the wilderness of uncertainties and errors like a camel suffering from night blindness. Under these circumstances it is best that you give up the quest because with such limitations none can ever reach the truth.

My dear son, carefully, very carefully remember these sayings of mine, that the Lord, who is the Master of death, is also the Master of life. The Creator is the Annihilator. And the One who annihilates has the power to bring everything back to existence again. The One who sends you calamities is the One who will bring you safely out of them.

Remember that this world is working under laws ordained by Him, and it consists of the totality of actions and reactions, causes and effects, calamities and reverses, pains and pleasures, rewards and punishment; but this is not all that the picture depicts; there are things in it that are beyond our understanding, things that we do not and cannot know, and things that cannot be foreseen and foretold. For instance, the rewards and punishments of the Day of Judgment. Under these circumstances, if you do not understand a thing, do not refuse to accept it. Remember that your lack of understanding is due to the insufficiency of your knowledge. Remember that when you came into this world, your first appearance was that of an ignorant, uneducated, and unlearned being; then you gradually acquired knowledge. There were several things in this world that were beyond your knowledge, which perplexed and surprised you and about which you did not understand "why" and "how"; gradually you acquired knowledge about some of those subjects, and in the future your knowledge and vision may further expand. Therefore, the best thing for you to do is to seek guidance of the One Who has created you, Who maintains and nourishes you, Who has given you a balanced mind and a normally working body. Your prayers should be reserved for Him only, your requests and solicitations should be to Him, you should be afraid of Him and of nobody else.

Be it known to you, my son, that no one has given mankind such detailed information about Allah, His Mercy, His Kindness, His Glory, His Might, and His Power, as did our Holy Prophet. I advise you to have faith in his teachings, to make him your leader, and to accept his guidance for your salvation. In thus advising you, I have done the best that I can do as a sincere and loving adviser, and I assure you that however you may try to find a better way for your good, you will not find any superior to the one advised by me for success in this world and salvation in the next. Remember, my son, that had there been any other god, beside the

147

One, he would also have sent his messengers and prophets, and they would have pointed out to mankind the domain and glory of this second god, and you would have seen them also. But no such incident ever took place. He is one God whom we all should recognize and worship. He has explained Himself. Nobody is a partner to Him in His Domain, His Might, and His Glory. He is Eternal, has always been, and shall always be. He existed before the universe came into being, but there is no beginning to His Existence. He shall remain when every other thing has disappeared into nothingness, and there shall be no end to His Existence. His Glory and His Existence are supreme, preeminent, transcendent, incomparable, and excellent—beyond the grasp of minds and intellects. None can understand or visualize Him. When you have accepted these truths and realities, then your behavior, as far as His orders and interdictions are concerned, should be that of a person who realizes that his status, power, and position are nothing when compared to that of his Lord, who wants to gain His favor through prayers and obedience, who fears His Wrath as well as His Punishments, and who is absolutely in need of His help and Protection. Remember, my son, that Allah has not ordered you to do anything but that which is good and propagates and distributes goodness, and He has not forbidden you anything but that which is bad and will bring about bad effects.

My dear son, through this message of mine, I have explained everything about this world, how fickle and quick-changing its attitude, how short-lived and evanescent is everything that it holds or offers, and how fast it changes its moods and its favors. I have also explained the life to come, the pleasures and blessings provided in it, and the everlasting peace, comfort, and happiness arranged for in Heaven. I have given enough examples of both aspects of life, before and after death, so that you may know the reality and lead your life on the basis of that knowledge.

The truth is that those people who have carefully studied the conditions of life and the world pass their days as if they know that they are travelers who have to leave a place that is barren, practically a desert almost devoid of food and water, unhealthy and uncongenial; and they have to go toward lands that are fertile, healthy, and congenial, and where there is abundant provision of all comforts and pleasures. They have eagerly taken up the journey, happy in the hope of future blessings and peace. They have willingly accepted the sufferings, troubles, and hazards of the way, the parting from friends, the scarcity of food and comfort during the pilgrimage, so that they may reach the journey's end—a happy place. They do not refuse to bear any discomfort and do not grudge any expense on the way, giving out alms and charities, and helping the poor and needy. Every step they put forward toward their goal, however tiring and exhausting it may be, is a happy event in their lives. On the contrary the condition of those people who are solely engrossed in this world and are sadly engulfed in its short-lived, quickly fading, and vicious pleasures, is like that of travelers who are staying in fertile and happy regions and who have to undertake a journey, knowing full well that the journey is going to end in inhospitable, arid, and infertile lands. Can anything be more loathsome to them than this journey? How they would hate to leave the place where they are and to arrive at the place that they so much hate and that is so dismaying, dreadful, and frightening.

My dear son, as far as your behavior with other human beings is concerned, let your "self" act as scales to help you judge its goodness or wickedness. Do unto others as you wish others to do unto you. Whatever you like for your "self," like for others, and whatever you dislike happening to you, spare others from. Do not oppress and tyrannize anyone, because you surely do not like to be oppressed and tyrannized. Be kind and sympathetic to others as you certainly desire others to treat you kindly and sympathetically. Whatever habits you find objectionable and loathsome in

149

others, abstain from developing. If you are satisfied or feel happy to receive a certain kind of behavior from others, then behave with others in exactly the same way. Do not speak about them in a way that you do not like others to speak about you. Do not speak on a subject about which you know little or nothing, and if you want to speak at all about anything or about anyone, then avoid scandal, libel, and aspersion yourself, for you would not like yourself to be scandalized and libeled.

Remember, son, that vanity and conceit are forms of folly, traits that will bring you serious harm and will be a constant source of danger to you. Lead a well-balanced life; neither be conceited nor suffer from the feeling that you are inferior, and exert yourself to earn an honest living. But do not act like a treasurer for somebody; do not be a miser who hoards what he earns. And whenever you receive guidance of the Lord to achieve the thing you desire, then do not be proud of your achievement but be humble and submissive to Him and realize that your success was due to His Mercy and Favor.

Remember, my son, that a long and arduous journey is before you. Life's journey is not only long, exhausting, laborious, and onerous, but the route is mostly through dismal, dreary, and deserted regions, where you will be sadly in need of refreshing and enlivening aids, and you cannot dispense with such provisions that will keep you going and maintain you to the end of your journey, the Day of Judgment. But remember not to overload yourself; do not entrust yourself with so many obligations and duties that you cannot honorably fulfill them, or burden yourself with a life so luxurious as to be wicked and vicious. Because if this load is more than you can conveniently bear, then your journey will be painful and toilsome. If you find around yourself poor, needy, and destitute people who are willing to carry your load as far as the Day of Judgment, then consider this to be a boon, engage them and pass your burden onto them. Distribute your wealth among the poor, destitute, and needy—help others to the best of your ability and be kind and sympathetic to human beings. Thus, relieve yourself of the heavy responsibility and liability of submitting an account on the day of reckoning of how you have made use of His Favors of health, wealth, power, and position. Thus you may arrive at the end of your journey light and fresh, and may have enough provision for you there, reward for having done your duty to man and Allah in this world. Have as many weight carriers as you can and help as many people as you can, so that you may have them when you need them. Remember that all you give out in charities and good deeds are like loans that will be paid back to you. Therefore when you are wealthy and powerful, make use of your wealth and power in such a way that you get all that back on the day when you will be poor and helpless: the Day of Judgment. Be it known to you, my son, that your passage lies through the dreadful valley of death, and the journey is extremely trying and arduous. Here a man with light weight is far better than an overburdened person, and one who can journey fast will pass through the valley more quickly than one whom encumberment forces to go slowly. You shall have to pass through this valley. The only way out of it is either in Heaven or in Hell; there is no other way out and no possibility of retracing your steps. Therefore, it is wise to send your things beforehand, so that your good actions arrive before you; prearrange the place of your stay before you reach it, because after death there is no repentance and no possibility of coming back to this world to undo the wrong done by you.

Realize this truth, my son, that the Lord Who owns and holds the treasure of the Heaven and earth has given you permission to ask and beg for it, and has promised to grant your prayers. He has told you to pray for His favors that they may be granted and to ask for His blessings that they may be bestowed. He has not appointed guards to keep your prayers from reaching Him. Nor is there any need for anybody to intercede with Him on your behalf.

151

If you go back upon your promises, if you break your vows or start doing things that you repent, He will not immediately punish you, neither will He refuse you His Favors and grant them in haste; and if you repent once again, He will neither taunt you nor betray you, though you may fully deserve both, but He will accept your repentance and forgive you. He never grudges His Forgiveness nor refuses His Mercy; on the contrary He has decreed repentance as a virtue and pious deed. The Merciful Lord has ordered that every evil deed of yours will be counted as one, and good deeds and pious actions will be rewarded tenfold. He has left the door of repentance open. He hears you whenever you call Him. He accepts your prayers whenever you pray to Him.

You beg of Him to grant you your heart's desires; you lay before Him the secrets of your heart; you tell Him about all the calamities that have befallen you and misfortunes that face you and beseech His Help to overcome them. You invoke His Help and Support in difficulties and distress. You implore Him to grant you long life and sound health; you pray to Him for prosperity, and you request of Him such favors and grants that none but He can bestow and award.

Think that by simply granting you the privilege of praying for His Favors and Mercies, He has handed over the keys of His Treasures to you. Whenever you are in need, you pray and He confers His Favors and Blessings.

But sometimes when you find that your requests are not immediately granted, then you need not be disappointed. Because the granting of prayers often rests with the true purpose and intention of the implorer. Sometimes the prayers are delayed because the Merciful Lord wants you to receive further rewards, to bear calamities and sufferings patiently, and still to believe sincerely in His Help. Thus you may be awarded better favors than you requested. Sometimes your prayers are turned down, and this is also in your interest; because you often, unknowingly, ask for things that are really harmful to you. If your requests are granted, they do more harm than good, and many of your requests may be such that, if granted, they would result in your eternal damnation. Thus the refusal to accede to your solicitations is a blessing in disguise to you. But very often your requests, if they are not really harmful to you in this world or in the hereafter, may be delayed, but they are granted in quantities much more than you had asked for, bringing in more blessings than you could ever imagine. So you should be very careful in asking Allah for His Favor; only pray for such things that are really beneficial to you, and these benefits are lasting, and in the long run they do not end in harm. Remember, my dear son, that wealth and power, if you pray for them, are such things that will not always be with you and may bring harm to you in the hereafter.

Be it known to you, my son, that you are created for the next world and not for this one. You are born to die and not to live forever. Your stay in this world is temporary. You live in a place that is subject to decay and destruction. It is a place where you will have to be busy getting ready for the next world. It is a road to the next world on which you are standing. Death is following you. You cannot run away from it. However hard you may try to avoid it, it is going to catch you sooner or later. Therefore take care that it may not catch you unaware and unprepared, and no chance is left to you to repent the vices and sins committed and undo the harm done by you. If death catches you unaware, then you are eternally damned. Therefore, my dear son, always keep three things in mind: death, your deeds and actions, and the life hereafter. In this way you will always be ready to face death, and it will not catch you unaware.

My dear son, do not be carried away and do not be allured by the infatuations of worldly people living a vicious life with its pleasures. Do not be impressed by the sight of their acute struggle to possess this world. Allah has mercifully explained to you

153

everything about this world, not only the Merciful Lord but this world has also told you everything; it has disclosed to you its mortality; it has openly declared its weakness, its shortcomings, and its vices.

Remember that these worldly people are barking dogs and hungry and ferocious beasts. Some of them are constantly barking at the others. Their mighty lords kill and massacre the poor and weak. Their powerful persons exploit and tyrannize the powerless. Their inordinate desires and their greed have such a complete hold over them that you will find some of them like animals tamed and tied with a rope around their feet and necks. They have lost freedom of thought and cannot come out of the enslavement of desires and habits. There are others whom wealth and power have turned mad. They behave like unruly beasts, trampling, crushing, and killing their fellow beings and destroying things around them. The history of this world is merely a record of such incidents, some big and some small; the difference is of might, but the intensity is the same. These people have lost the balance of their minds. They do not know what they are doing and where they are going; scan their activities and study their ways of thinking—you will find them confused and irrational. They appear like cattle wandering in a dreary desert where there is no water to drink and no food to eat, no shepherd to care for them and no guardian to look after them. What has actually happened to them is that the vicious world has taken possession of them; it is dragging them wherever it likes and is treating them as if they are blind, because it has in reality blindfolded them against the divine light of true religion. They are wandering without true aims and sober purposes in the wonderful show that the world has staged for them; they are drunk with the wine and pleasures amassed around them. They take this world to be their god and nourisher. The world is playing with them, and they are playing with it, and have forgotten and forsaken everything else.

154

But the nights of enjoyment and pleasures will not last forever for anybody; the dawn of realities will break sooner or later. The caravan of life will surely reach its destination one day. One who has night and day acting as piebald horses for him, carrying him onward and onward toward his journey's end, must remember that, though he may feel as if he is stopping at one place, actually he is moving on, he is en route to his destination. Every day is carrying him a step further in his journey toward death.

Be it known to you, my son, that you cannot have every wish of yours granted, you cannot expect to escape death, and you are passing through your days of life as others before you have done. Therefore control your expectations, desires, and cravings; be moderate in your demands; earn your livelihood through scrupulously honest means; be contented with what you get honestly and honorably; go slow and do not let your desires drive you madly, because there are many desires that will lead you toward disappointments and loss. Remember that every beggar or everyone who prays for a thing will not always get what he begs or prays for, and everyone who controls his desires, has self-respect, and does not beg or pray for things will not always remain unlucky or disappointed. So, do not bring down your self-respect; do not be mean and submissive, and do not subjugate yourself through vile and base traits, though they may appear to make it possible for you to achieve your heart's desires; because nothing in this world can compensate for the loss of self-respect, nobleness of mind, and honor.

Take care, my son; be warned that you do not make yourself a slave of anyone. Allah has created you a free man. Do not sell your freedom in return for anything. There is no actual gain or real value in benefits that you derive from selling your honor and self-respect or from subjugating yourself to disgrace, insults, and indignities. There is no real good in wealth and power acquired by foul means. Beware, my son, lest avarice and greed drive you toward destruction and damnation. If you can succeed in having only Allah as your benefactor, He will grant you your share whether or not you try to gather around you donors, patrons, and benefactors.

Remember that the little given to you by Allah is going to be more useful, serviceable, honorable, and respectable than what is granted by man in copious and abundant quantities. What can a man give you but part of that which Allah has granted him?

The losses that you suffer on account of your silence can be easily compensated for, but the losses that arise out of excessive and loose talk are difficult to requite. Do you not see that the best way of guarding water in a water bay is to close its mouth?

To guard what you already possess is better than to ask and pray for what others possess.

The bitterness of disappointment, privation, and poverty is actually sweeter than the disgrace and humiliation of begging.

The returns from hard but respectable and honorable labor of a craft or profession, though small in quantity, are better than the wealth acquired through sin and wickedness.

Nobody can guard your secrets better than you.

Often a man tries his best to acquire a thing that is most harmful to him. Often we do ourselves the worse harm.

One who talks too much makes most mistakes.

One who often thinks and reflects develops his foresight and vision.

By keeping the company of good people, you will develop goodness in your character, and by avoiding the company of wicked persons you will abstain from wickedness.

Livelihood acquired by foul means is the worst form of livelihood.

To oppress a weak and helpless person is the worst form of tyranny and wickedness.

If your kindness or indulgence is going to bring forth cruel results, then severity or strictness is the real kindness.

Often, medicating results in disease; sometimes diseases prove

156

to be health preservers.

Often you obtain warnings and advice from people who are not fit to warn and advise you, and often you will come across advisers who are not sincere.

Do not rely on vain hopes, because vain hopes are the assets of idiots and fools.

Wisdom is the name of the trait of remembering experiences and making use of them. The best experience is the one that gives the best warning and advice.

Take advantage of opportunities before they turn their backs upon you.

Everyone who tries cannot succceed.

Everyone who goes out of this world will not come back.

The worst form of folly is to waste the opportunities of this life and to lose salvation.

For every action there is a reaction.

Shortly you will get what has been destined for you.

There is an element of risk and speculation in every trade as well as danger of loss.

Often small returns prove as beneficial as big profits.

An accessory or accomplice who insults you, and a friend who has not formed a good opinion of you will not be of any help or use to you.

Treat with consideration and kindness those over whom you have power and authority.

Do not run the risk of endangering yourself through irrational, unreasonable, and extravagant hopes.

Take care and do not be fooled by flattery.

Do good to your brother when he is bent upon doing harm to you. When he ignores or declines to recognize the kinship, befriend him, go to his help, and try to maintain relations. If he is miserly and refuses monetary help, be generous with him and support him financially. If he is harsh and cruel, be kind and considerate with him. If he harms you, accept his excuses. Behave with him as if he is a master and you are a slave, and he is a benefactor and you are a beneficiary. But be careful that you do not behave thus with undeserving and mean persons.

Do not develop friendship with the enemy of your friend; otherwise your friend will turn into an enemy.

Advise your friend sincerely and to the best of your ability, though he may not like it.

Keep a complete control over your temper and anger, because I have never found anything more beneficial at the end and more productive of good results than such control.

Be mild, pleasant, and lenient with him who is harsh, gross, and strict with you; gradually he will turn to your way of behavior.

Grant favor and be considerate of your enemy, because you will thus gain either one or the other of the two kinds of victories: one, rising above your enemy; the other, reducing the intensity of his enmity.

If you want to cease relations with your friend, then do not break off totally; let your heart retain some consideration for him, so that you still have some regard for him if he comes back to you.

Do not disappoint a person who holds a good opinion of you, and do not make him change his opinion.

Under the impression that you, as a friend, can behave as you like, do not violate the rights of your friend, because when deprived of his rights and privilege, he will no longer remain your friend.

Do not ill-treat members of your household and do not behave with them as if you are the worst-tempered and the most cruel man alive.

Do not run after him who tries to avoid you.

The greatest achievement of your character is that the enmity of your brother against you dare not overcome the consideration and friendship you feel toward him, and his ill-treatment of you cannot overbalance your kind treatment to him.

Do not get too worried and depressed over oppressions and cruelties, because whoever oppresses you or tyrannizes you is in reality doing himself harm.

Never ill-treat a person who has done good unto you.

Know it well, son, that there are two kinds of livelihood: one that you are searching for and the other, which has been destined for you, that will reach you even if you do not try to obtain it.

To be submissive, humble, crawling, and begging when one is needy, powerless, and poor, and to be arrogant, oppressing, and cruel when in power and opulence are two very ugly traits of human character.

Nothing in this world is really useful and beneficial to you unless it has some utility and benefit value for you in the next world. If you want to lament over things that you have lost in this world, then worry and feel sorry over the loss of things that had immortal values for you.

The past and almost all that was in your possession during the past is not with you now. You may thus rationally come to the conclusion that the present and all that is in your possession will also leave you.

Do not be like persons on whom advice has no effect and who require punishment to correct this. A sensible and reasonable man acquires education and culture through advice, and brutes and beasts always accept correction through punishment and chastisement.

Overcome your sorrows, worries, and misfortunes through hard work, patience, and faith in the Merciful Lord; one who gives up a straight path, honest and rational ways of thinking and working, will harm himself.

A friend is like a relation, and a true friend is one who speaks well of you even behind your back.

Inordinate desires have close relations with misfortunes and calamities.

Often close relatives behave more distantly than strangers, and often strangers help you more than your nearest relatives.

Poor is he who has no friends. Whoever forsakes truth finds that his path of life has become narrow and troublesome.

He who wants to retain his prestige and position, through contentment and honesty, will find them lasting assets.

The strongest relation is the one between man and Allah.

One who does not care for you is your enemy.

If there is a danger of death or damnation in achievement of an object, then your safety lies in your failure to achieve it.

Weaknesses and shortcomings are not the things to talk about.

Opportunities do not repeat themselves.

Sometimes wise and learned persons fail to achieve the object they aim for, and foolish and uneducated people attain their purposes.

Postpone evil deeds as long as possible because you can commit them whenever you so desire.

To sever your connections with ignorant and uneducated people is itself like keeping company with wise and learned persons.

Whoever trusts this world is betrayed by it, and whoever gives it importance and exalts its position is disgraced and humiliated by it.

Every arrow of yours will not hit the bull's eye.

With a change of status and position, your condition will also change.

Before ascertaining the condition of a route, find out what kind of persons will accompany you on the journey.

Instead of inquiring about the condition of a home in which you are going to stay, first of all try to find out what kind of people your neighbors are.

Do not introduce ridiculous topics in your talk even if you have to repeat sayings of others.

Divide and distribute work among your servants so that you can hold each one responsible for the work entrusted to him. This is a better and smoother way of carrying on work than giving each servant the opportunity to throw work on somebody else.

Treat the members of your family with love and respect, because they act as wings with which you fly, and as hands that support you and fight for you. They are people toward whom you turn when in trouble and in need.

My dear son, after having given this advice, I entrust you to the Lord. He will help, guide, and protect you in this world and the hereafter. I pray and beseech Him to take you under His protection in both worlds.

As one looked ahead, one could only see the *taj*, the golden turban of the sheikh, resting on the coffin. . . . It seemed as though Sheikh Muzaffer in all his splendor was leading these thousands of people. May Allah be pleased with him. . . .